Indian *for* Everyone

100 EASY, HEALTHY DISHES THE WHOLE FAMILY WILL LOVE

Hari Ghotra

FAIR WINDS

Contents

Introduction

WHEN MY EDITOR first suggested the title of this book, I thought it was a bit obvious—*of course* Indian food is for everyone! But if you've never had much exposure to spice, or if you're worried it will be complex and time-consuming to cook Indian food, I'm here to set the record straight. Indian food is actually not that complicated, and the flavors and techniques can add new dimensions to standard British or American fare, at any meal (even breakfast). So maybe you're a mom or dad looking for a quick, healthy weeknight dinner or planning an elaborate family feast. Maybe you like the idea of using spices, but you're a little unsure about where to start. Or maybe you are looking for fun ideas for a glam dinner party with your friends, a fresh and fiery barbecue, or a tasty vegetarian (or vegan) spread. It could even be that you are feeling a little under the weather and need a warming, spicy pick-me-up to give you a hug from the inside out.

Whatever the case, these are some of my favorite recipes, which illustrate how you can make Indian flavors part of your everyday life (and special occasions, of course!). The recipes in this book are unique in that they blend the influence of my family and ancestors with the tricks I have picked up. I hope your confidence increases and you'll feel inspired to make these dishes on your own.

IT ALL STARTS WITH A LITTLE SPICE

If you've never cooked with spices, I hope this book gives you the confidence to start. Understanding what they do and how to use them will forever change the way you view food.

Spices are not just about flavor and aromatics; in Indian cooking their contributions are much more holistic: They can be used to delicately soothe and aid digestion, induce an internal cooling or warming sensation, stimulate the immune system, and so much more—the delicious taste they infuse doesn't hurt either. Once you pluck up the courage to get started, I've even given you some red-hot tips on how to crank up the punchiness for those who love a kick, and how to mellow things down for those with a more delicate palate. I have also tried to show you how you can adjust the dishes for people with differing dietary requirements.

If you are a novice when cooking Indian food or an old hand, there is always something new to try. Indian food continues to evolve as new influences, new ideas, and new cooking techniques come to the scene.

As a British-born Indian, I have seen how Indian food has been adopted into everyday life in the U.K. As a nation we love Indian cuisine; the United Kingdom is probably the most advanced Western country in its journey and love affair with the cuisine. Being lucky enough to travel the world with my job, I have realized that the flavors I am used to at home are now impacting all parts of the world in so many different cuisines. They are now familiar to so many people, and having a curry or an Indian meal (as exciting as it is) is becoming part of their everyday repertoire.

THE INDIAN MEAL

Contrary to what you may occasionally experience at your local takeout joint, the Indian meal isn't about filling a hunger hole with a monotonous starter, a huge mountain of curry and rice, and then a sweet dessert. Rather, it's about indulging the senses, experiencing a flow of energy to satisfy the mind, soul, and body by reinvigorating each and every cell with nutrients, exciting visual cues, and an elevated physical dining experience. The meal usually consists of a multitude of small dishes, each embellished differently with condiments and spices—a surfeit of vivid colors and indulgent flavors that wrap around your tongue and excite each and every one of your senses.

In Indian culture, your home is your personal temple, a sacred place where any guest is welcomed and always treated like a god. You are blessed to have them in your life, and you honor them by breaking bread together. Hospitality, kindness, and love are what mealtimes are all about—chatting, laughing, exploring flavors, and, most of all, sharing all that you have with others. Indians love to savor food, so we eat slowly and we reflect, which is why variety is important at every mealtime.

THE INDIAN DINNER PARTY

The process of Indian dining at home is very different from the West, mostly in terms of timing.

A gathering always begins with a cup of sweet tea or a drink, and a few shared treats. Then it's all about snacks, nibbles, chutneys, dips, and sharing platters for the next couple of hours. The main meal comes much later in the evening, and it is usually a selection of small tapas-style dishes served together, representing all the different food groups (proteins, carbohydrates, dairy, fats, vegetables). These might include a meat or fish curry, vegetable masalas, lentil dhals, rice and/or breads, a yogurt-based raita, and a fresh salad or kachumber. The meal may or may not end with something sweet, but if so, it's usually something light like sliced and spiced fruit. And then, before bed, the aim is to end each and every day with something special to settle you into a great night of rest.

Happily (for me), we seem to be moving away from the stiff fine-dining approach across cultures. The new ideal is to gather your loved ones in a relaxed environment and focus on enjoying yourselves rather than worrying about using the correct spoon or fork. Indian dining has always been more about people and the food rather than the formalities.

FIVE FINGERS, FIVE ELEMENTS

The art of eating with your hands is a precise and delicate practice inspired by Ayurvedic teachings. Each finger is said to be an extension of one of the five elements of nature. The thumb is an extension of space, the forefinger air, the middle finger fire, the ring finger water, and the little finger earth. When eating, your fingers bring together all of nature's elements and heighten your awareness of the texture, taste, aromas, and temperature of the food, making the whole experience not just about fuel for the body but also fuel for the senses. When you touch your food with your hands, you are creating a physical and spiritual connection with it becoming more present in the moment.

INDIAN FOOD AROUND THE WORLD

Just like people, food doesn't stand still—it is constantly evolving and changing. Outside influences, ingredients, cooks, and communities all contribute to this evolution. So often, we get caught up in the idea of "authenticity" that we lose sight of the most important thing: that cooking and eating is all about bringing people together, to share, smile, and enjoy.

The migration of Indians across the globe is a complex and diverse story that cannot be thoroughly covered. Since about the nineteenth century it's thought that ethnic Indians have set up established communities in every continent in the world and on islands as far-reaching as the Caribbean, the Pacific, and the

Indian oceans. This flow of migrants evolved over the years starting mainly with indentured labor in colonies from the Caribbean and West Indies to the post-war labor workforce pulled in for British industries. High-skilled professionals such as doctors and lawyers were drawn into North America whereas laborers and low-skilled workers went to work in the Middle East. This initial movement of Indians has also been further embellished by a secondary migration movement from African countries such as Kenya to other areas.

With all of this movement, familiar food, recipes, and cooking methods migrate as well, as these are part of one's identity. Along the journey, dishes are adapted using new local ingredients, merged with new recipes and cooking methods. Through future generations and changes in their tastes, new creations come into being, and food from India has seen this growth in many ways.

Throughout my childhood I can remember my parents desperately trying to replicate the outdoor cooking techniques they used in India to recapture the flavors of their childhood and remind them of home. Every year my dad would collect various bits of equipment, from oil drums to clay to wire mesh, and each summer he and my mum would set about making an outdoor oven. We didn't understand why they couldn't just cook the chicken in the perfectly good oven in the kitchen, but every year they came up with a new contraption and every year we would enjoy burned tandoori chicken in the garden. Sometimes it was covered in ash as it had fallen into the burning charcoal, and one year the concrete my dad used cracked and the whole drum collapsed, but they were never disheartened. Having never seen a tandoor oven, we thought the oldies were losing the plot, but they were happy reliving cooking experiences from their village.

Curry is a prime example of food evolution, and like all progress, it can be polarizing; even the word "curry" itself is controversial. People have told me they feel it's disrespectful, because it reduces a whole culinary heritage and complex craft into a single dish. As much as I understand the sentiment, I also think that the challenge of communicating the diversity of food from the Indian subcontinent, as the cuisine became more and more popular in Western cultures, would be

well near impossible. The flavors of India have slowly filtered across the world over many years, so it makes sense to me to use a shorthand that people immediately understand. But I can agree, at least, that the word "curry" seems lazy in today's food world, where there's so much more awareness of the variances and regionality within Indian food.

The idea that Indian food is only about hot and spicy simply isn't true. Indian cooking is about building aromatic layers of flavor through different cooking techniques and by using spices. Adding spices to your cooking is a great way to add interest to your meals and to get kids used to new flavor profiles. I use spices in all different styles of food and even in dishes you wouldn't normally expect to see them—all cuisines can benefit from them. So please do not be put off because you don't like heat—you can always skip the chillies!

TIPS FOR COOKING AN INDIAN CURRY

When preparing any dish, I first think about what I am hoping to end up with because then I know what I need to do during the cooking process to achieve that outcome. Am I looking for a deep, dark, moody meat curry or a light, fragrant fish curry or a dry vegetable side dish? Once you have the answer, you will be able to define the ingredients you need, how to prepare them, and how to cook the dish to achieve the desired goal.

"It's all about the onions!" Many (though not all) Indian dishes start with onions, to make a basic masala. Before we cook our onions, it's important to get them chopped to the right shape and size for your dish—are you looking for a smooth, creamy sauce or a chunky one? This will define whether you slice, chop, grate, or blitz your onions.

How you brown your onions can also make or break your dish. When I teach my cooking classes, I tell my students that Indian food is all about how you treat your onions. A deep, dark curry requires the onions to be cooked down until they are soft and dark, which gives you not only the color you are looking for but also the depth of flavor. There are two main ways to effectively brown your onions: a low, slow cook during which the onion cells break down to make a paste; or at a higher temperature during which the onions brown more quickly, resulting in browned onions that still have texture and shape.

Technically when we cook our onions like this, we are not caramelizing them because they don't contain enough sugar to reach the temperatures required for caramelization. We are browning them through the Maillard process during which there's a reaction between the sugars, carbohydrates, amino acids, and heat, resulting in a complex meaty flavor as the onions cook.

Choose onions that are pungent—brown/yellow or white—as these will brown better because they have higher sulfur compounds than a less pungent onion, such as a red onion.

- For a deep, dark, slow-cooked meat dish, gently cook your onions to a dark brown color until the onion starts to break down. Start on a high heat to disperse the moisture. Reduce the heat and stir the onions until a dark brown color is achieved, adding a splash of water every time the onions stick to the pan.

- For a light vegetable or lentil dish in which you want the vegetables to sing, the onions need to be cooked only until they are a wonderfully golden brown color.

- For a white masala or a fish dish that's light and fresh, the onions are cooked only until translucent or just starting to color.

MAKING INDIAN FOR EVERYONE

Here are a few easy tips you can use to ensure the Indian meals you cook are suitable for everyone in the family, whatever their age, dietary requirement, likes, or dislikes.

Children

Get them eating spices early—I weaned my kids on Kitcheree, which is a delicate lentil and rice porridge that's easy to digest but still flavorful.

For young kids, dial down the salt, chillies, and garlic.

Most kids love breads, so naans, rotis, and parathas are a great way to get them dipping into sauces and chutneys.

Kids love food they can pick up, so finger foods like kebabs and pakora are great.

If you involve your children in the cooking of a dish, they will be more likely to try it.

It doesn't have to be hot to be tasty. So if you are cooking for children (or someone who doesn't like hot food), remove or tone down the number of chillies you use during cooking, or separate out portions without chillies.

I find children are often put off by different textures. My kids used to dislike chunks of onions, so I would make the masala and then purée their portion.

Add a little creaminess and sweetness with yogurt, cream, or coconut milk. If anyone has a problem with lactose, instead soak almonds or cashews in boiling water until they soften, and then blend to a purée before adding to the dish.

Vegetarians

Indian food is a great option for vegetarians because the masalas and spice add a depth of flavor that works well with many different vegetables.

Dhal, beans, and legumes are great with spices, and they are a fantastic source of protein. But be sure you know exactly what you are using so you cook it long enough.

In most of my recipes, you can replace the meat with vegetables. If it's a long, slow-cooked dish, choose vegetables that will hold up to a longer cooking time, even though you will still need to reduce the cooking time.

There are lots of unique Indian vegetables that I would urge you to try, from okra to snake beans, karela to tindora—just do a little research on the best way to prepare them.

Vegan or Plant-Based Diets

The Indian diet is superb if you are vegan because it uses a vast array of beans, lentils, and legumes as well as vegetables.

Many masalas are vegan already, so they require very little manipulation.

Milk-based elements are common in Indian cuisine—namely ghee, yogurts, and raita. But most dishes work just fine with standard milk substitutes. Here are my suggestions:

- Replace ghee/butter with coconut oil.

- To make raita or dips, replace yogurt with the many dairy-free alternatives that are now available.

- To replace cream, use coconut cream/milk or a cornstarch slurry made with a nondairy milk and a touch of maple syrup.

- To thicken sauces, use nut pastes made by soaking nuts and blending them with a nondairy milk.

- Paneer can be replaced with soya protein, tempeh, or tofu.

- Get familiar with aquafaba, or bean water (the water from a tin of chickpeas); it whips up like egg whites and can be used to make mayonnaise and even meringues.

Gluten Free

Most Indian dishes are naturally gluten free. Spices, basic masalas, and sauces are already free from ingredients containing gluten. Sauces are not usually thickened using wheat flours either.

Indian breads like roti, poori, and naan are naturally the most challenging for a gluten-free diner, as they are made with wheat flour. There are many wheat-free flours you can try. I have experimented with different brands to varying success, but the results are different as they come out more like flatbreads rather than the puffy breads we are used to. Alternative options include:

- breads/pancakes made using gram flour—chilla, pudla

- crepes made using lentil or rice batters—dosa, idli

- breads made using fermented rice batters—idli, appam

Allium Intolerance

More common than you think, allium intolerance causes the body to launch an immune response resulting in severe digestive problems. This intolerance can be triggered when onions, garlic, spring onions, leeks, or chives are consumed. The only way to manage it is through avoiding these items in your diet. You may think that this means Indian food is out, but that's not true. There is a segment of the Hindu religion who are known as Jains. They believe in total nonviolence, which includes what they eat—no meat and no plants that are extracted from the ground (potatoes, onions, garlic, and so on) as they would be able to continue growing. They consume only berries, legumes, and fruits that do not harm the plant when picked. There are a number of things you can do to ensure you have a nice, flavorful meal without garlic or onions.

Asafoetida is the dried, powdered resin that comes from the sap of a giant fennel-like plant that grows in Iran. It has a bitter, acrid flavor and smells really awful when raw, but once fried it gives a wonderful aroma and the flavor profile of onions and garlic to your dish. It should be used only in tiny amounts as it is very pungent. You treat it as a whole spice and add it to hot oil at the start of the cooking process. It's used in lentil and vegetable dishes to give the pungency of onions when they are not present in the recipe. Used a lot in Kashmiri, Maharashtrian, and South Indian cooking, it is known to have many health benefits, including its anti-flatulence properties and its ability to soothe digestive problems.

If you have an intolerance to onions, other options that give you the texture and body of an onion include fennel, carrots, celery, and even parsnips. If you don't like onions and need something milder, then shallots or spring onions are also an option.

Here is an example of how you use asafoetida in a traditional curry.

Lamb Rogan Josh

Serves 4-6

2 tablespoons (30 ml) mustard oil

large pinch asafoetida

1 teaspoon cumin seeds

1 stick of cassia bark

3 cloves

2 whole dried Kashmiri chillies

2 black cardamom pods

2 green cardamom pods

1 teaspoon salt

2 pounds (800 g) leg of lamb, cut into large chunks

1 teaspoon red Kashmiri chilli powder
(or ratanjot, if you have it)

1 teaspoon hot chilli powder (optional)

1 teaspoon ginger powder

1 teaspoon fennel powder

3 heaped tablespoons (45 g) Greek yogurt

3 to 4 tablespoons (50 ml) water

1 teaspoon garam masala

In a wide pan, heat the mustard oil on high heat to smoking point before removing from the heat. Allow it to cool; then reheat on low heat and add the asafoetida. Once it sizzles, add all the whole spices—cumin seeds, cassia, cloves, dried chillies, black and green cardamoms—and salt to taste.

Once the spices become fragrant, add the meat and fry until it turns a lovely brown color. Reduce the heat, add the chilli powders (or ratanjot, if you have it), and let the meat cook for a few minutes (leave on a low heat so the chilli powder doesn't burn).

Add the ginger and fennel powders.

Stir in the yogurt 1 tablespoon at a time. Once mixed through, place the lid on the pan and leave on the lowest heat setting to gently simmer for up to an hour. Check after 30 minutes and add some water if needed, leaving to cook until the meat is tender.

Once the meat is tender, add enough boiling water to cover the meat to create a lovely gravy. Allow it to simmer gently for 5–7 minutes, and then add the garam masala and serve.

Nightshade Intolerance

I often get asked about nightshade intolerance in my line of work, usually referring to tomatoes. The likelihood is that if you are intolerant to tomatoes, you will have an intolerance to potatoes, eggplants, and even latex. This intolerance is known to cause digestive issues but also other issues ranging from joint pain, stiffness, headaches, nausea, and even skin irritations. To avoid tomatoes in your diet, you can select curries without tomatoes such as Korma, dry vegetable dishes, and rogan josh. You can substitute the tomatoes for yogurt to add tartness and a silky mouth feel.

If you just don't like tomatoes, another option is to roast or blacken red peppers , and then blitz them to a paste to add depth. Many dishes that traditionally include tomatoes can also be cooked successfully without them.

ALL ABOUT SPICES

We talk about spices all the time, but do you actually know what they are? Spices are vegetative substances—a fruit, a seed, bark, or even skin—that are used in small quantities as food additives to enhance (or hide!) flavors, to add color, or to preserve. These little gems also have many other properties that can be used in medicine, cosmetics, and perfumery. For example, cloves contain a chemical called eugenol that inhibits the growth of bacteria, and the active agent in turmeric is curcumin, which is responsible not only for its bright yellow color but for its effectiveness as an anti-inflammatory.

As a result, many spices are routinely used in various forms of alternative medicine.

PROPERTIES OF SPICES

Different spices have warming or cooling effects on our bodies. Just as Mother Earth gives us specific plants at certain times of the year so our bodies can get the nutrients they need, so are spices used seasonally in Indian cooking. For example, dishes that contain mustard seeds are prepared when the season is changing and we are more prone to colds, because

mustard seeds contain minerals that help to ward off these bugs.

Spices come in either a whole form (in their natural state) or ground to a powder. It is always best to go with whole spices and grind them yourself when you need them, if possible. This way they will retain their natural oils for longer, and therefore retain their flavor-enhancing properties.

USING SPICES

The way you use spices matters. Depending on whether they are roasted, ground, boiled, or crushed, they will give a slightly different aromatic. With spices, less is more, and small amounts can have a huge impact on the dish you are cooking. If you are a novice, start with something gentle like cumin, and as you experiment more, you will discover which flavors you like.

To determine how and when spices should be added, I categorize them into groups based on when they are added to the pan. This should give you a framework to use spices more effectively and also allow your dishes to have that delicate layering of flavor that curries are known for.

Stage 1: Base—Whole Spices

These are generally tempered, which means they are heated in hot oil (or dry fried) at the beginning of the cooking process to release their natural oils gradually. Whole spices include cassia bark, green cardamom, cloves, cumin seeds, mustard seeds, and bay leaves. They form the base flavor of your dish and are added at the beginning. Not every dish requires whole spices, especially simple ones.

Stage 2: Vibrancy—Taste and Color Spices

These are added to the pan one at a time, usually mid-way through the recipe. They typically come in powder form, meaning the oils are released more readily, so you don't want to add them at the start, as the aromatics will dissipate too quickly. They should also be added to a liquid base, to prevent them from burning. So once the tomatoes, yogurt, or coconut milk has

gone in, the ground spices go in. This group includes chilli, coriander, cumin, and turmeric.

Stage 3: Finesse—Delicate Aromatic Spices

These are the more delicate spices such as cardamom, mace, or garam masala—powders that are added at the end of the cooking process. These enhance the final flavor profiles and add the final aromas of the dish. Delicate herbs, like fresh coriander and dried fenugreek (methi), will also go in at the end.

STORING SPICES

Spices are natural ingredients, and the purpose of using them is to harness their natural oils. So it's important that we keep those vital oils inside as long as possible. Generally, whole spices, if stored correctly, will keep fresh for nine to twelve months. Ground spices, if stored correctly, will keep for six to nine months.

Here is my advice:

- Store spices in airtight containers in a dark space, not near a heat source.

- Invest in an Indian masala dabba, which is a spice box that is dark and airtight; plus it keeps all your spices in one place.

- Buy spices whole and grind them when required.

- Taste and smell your spices to judge if they are fresh.

TEN KEY SPICES

Cumin Seeds (Jeera)

These brown oval seeds can be used whole or ground and will give a warming pungent flavor. Beautifully aromatic, cumin brings out the natural sweetness of a dish. When used whole, they add a nutty flavor and texture. I always buy cumin whole and crush it as needed. It's also known to be high in iron and to help relieve digestive problems.

Coriander Seeds (Dhania)

These round, beige seeds are warming and fragrant when crushed. The seeds release a gentle citrus flavor almost like lemon or orange. They are known to help reduce cholesterol and have a cooling effect on the body. If you suffer from nasal congestion, you could boil a teaspoon of coriander seeds in a mug of water, strain, cool, and drink to help relieve the tension.

Planting these seeds will result in a beautiful coriander plant with very delicate, highly perfumed flat leaves that give off a light freshness. The flavor is completely different from that of the coriander seeds, so do not substitute one for the other.

Turmeric (Haldi)

Related to ginger, turmeric is a root that is dried and ground to create a bright yellow powder (the iconic "curry" color). It has a chalky texture and a woody aroma with slightly bitter undertones. It's well known in the Indian world as a super spice for its antiseptic and anti-inflammatory properties. Recently it has also gone mainstream; you can find it in everything from cereals to coffees.

Chillies (Mirch)

The many varieties can be used fresh or sun-dried, whole or ground to a powder. Fresh green finger chillies are the chilli of choice to add heat and freshness. My preferred variety of chilli powder is Kashmiri, as it's mild and gives a gentle, smoked warmth, plus a beautifully vibrant red color. All chilli powders are different—some can be smoky and others much more fiery—so it's a good idea to know what you are using.

Dried Fenugreek Leaves (Kasoori Methi)

The herb and the seed are two very different ingredients, and it's not a great idea to substitute the spice for the herb. The green powder, or dried green herb, is made from the leaves of the plant. Used to flavor lamb and lentil dishes, it has a very characteristic, musky "curry" aroma with a slight bitter taste. Young fresh leaves are used as greens, more like spinach. Fenugreek seeds are beige in color and look like little stones. They can be ground down to a powder and have a very strong, bitter, earthy flavor. Using too much of the ground seeds when cooking can be very overpowering; you only need half a teaspoon for a meal serving eight people.

Garam Masala

Literally, "garam" means warm, and "masala" is a spice blend. An aromatic blend of spices, it usually contains cumin, black pepper, coriander seeds, cassia bark, carom seeds, black cardamom, cloves, green cardamom, and bay leaves, which leaves a delicate warming sensation. Indian families often have their own special blend of garam masala, and so do I. Garam masala is probably one of the most important ingredients in northern Indian food, usually added at the end of the cooking process to intensify and refresh all the flavors and fragrances of the dish.

Mustard Seeds (Sarson)

These come in three varieties—white, brown, or black. When these tiny round seeds are heated, they release a unique nose-tingling pungency, like that of horseradish. Indian cooking generally uses black or brown seeds. It's a harsh spice great for pickles and achaar in vegetable and lentil dishes. A great combination for Indian vegetable dishes is cumin and mustard; together, they offer both warmth and bite. High in magnesium, mustard seeds are known to assist in lowering blood pressure and aiding digestion.

Cassia Bark (Dal Chini) and Cinnamon

Cassia bark is related to cinnamon, but it isn't the same. Cassia adds a sweeter, milder flavor, whereas cinnamon has a stronger, harsher, hotter flavor. Cassia originated in Southeast Asia from one tree variety called *Cinnamomum*, which is known as Chinese or true cinnamon. It is thicker, like the outer bark of a tree, and darker in color. Most other cinnamon comes from related species that are generally referred to as cassia.

Cinnamon is lighter beige in color and made up of wafer-thin quills. Most of the world's cinnamon quills are produced in Sri Lanka. Cassia is usually cheaper than cinnamon as very little labor is required to produce it, whereas cinnamon quills require a workforce. For all my Indian dishes, I use cassia rather than cinnamon.

Both are used in desserts as well as savory and rice dishes. In those lighter, sweeter dishes such as a Korma or Pasanda, it gives the very subtle sweetness that these dishes are known for.

Cloves (Laung)

These are dried flower pods that look like miniature black scepters. They have a very strong, distinct flavor that comes from the chemical eugenol, so they should be used sparingly. In any one dish you would only need three or four of them. Cloves leave a warming sensation and are generally used in dishes both sweet and savory alongside their sister spice, green cardamom. Cloves are also known to have anti-microbial properties and a numbing quality—they were once used to dull the pain of toothaches.

Green Cardamom (Elachi)

These are small green pods, each containing about twenty black seeds. They are commonly used in traditional Indian sweets, desserts, Indian chai, and savory meat dishes. Green cardamom is also an important ingredient in some spice blends. The pods themselves are quite fibrous, but they can be ground down to a powder or used whole, or you can remove the husk and pound the seeds. They have a bittersweet flavor and an intense aromatic perfume that people usually either love or hate. You would only use three or four pods at a time, and they should be stored whole, because once the seeds are exposed, they lose their aromatics very quickly. Ensure your cardamom pods are green when you use them, as it's the green color that indicates they have the desired aromatics in them. After a meal many people chew on the pods, which act like a breath freshener. They are also known to help break up gallstones and kidney stones.

CLASSIC INDIAN COOKING TECHNIQUES

The essence of Indian cooking is to infuse aromatics and flavors into your dish in a way that raises the dining experience.

There are a number of classic Indian cooking techniques used in authentic Indian stovetop cooking. Used differently for various dishes, they all play a part in infusing a dish with flavor and aromatics.

Tadka (Tempering)

Tadka, baghar, and chowkna are all the same principle but called different things in different regions. Known

A NOTE ABOUT CURRY POWDER:

This is an all-in-one spice blend that gives a very generic curry taste. It's not used by Indian cooks to make curry because they would always use the individual spices specific to the dish being cooked. In the United Kingdom, curry powder was an ingenious way for Brits who had lived in India during the Raj (when India was under British rule from 1858 to 1947) to bring the flavors of the East and the cuisine they had come to adore back to "Blighty" in an easy-to-use format. There is no real recipe to make it, but a mild one generally includes cumin, coriander, and turmeric; a hot curry powder may include chilli powder; and a madras includes black pepper, mustard, and ginger. Other commercial blends may also include clove, cardamom, bay leaf, and fenugreek. Curry powder is used across the globe to give the desired aromas to curry dishes from the Caribbean, Japan, Mauritius, and China, and it's now a basic kitchen ingredient around the world.

in English as tempering, this method is about infusing whole spices in hot oil or ghee to intensify their natural flavors and to create a fragrant oil that is used either at the beginning of the cooking process, for the base flavor of the dish, or as the final garnish, as with some dhals and chutneys.

Bhuna or Bhuno (Stir-Fry to Reduce)

This method is a mixture of stir-frying and sautéing: sautéing and browning (usually onions) over a low-and-slow heat at the start of the cooking process, creating real depth and intensity for the base masala, then letting the onions just melt away into the sauce. You can also bhun meat dishes at the end of the cooking time over a high heat; this intensifies the flavor and reduces the sauce until it clings to the meat.

Dhum or Dum (Steam Infusion)

This method is essentially steaming or simmering on very low heat over a long cooking period in a vessel that is sealed closed. The process allows the ingredients to cook in their own juices and, if cooking meat on the bone, the marrow renders out to pack the dish full of flavor. The results of this method are very close to those achieved by a slow cooker.

This is the traditional technique (two hundred years old) of cooking a biryani known as dum pukht, where rice and spiced meat are layered in a round-bottomed clay or metal vessel called a handi. By trapping the steam inside, it allowed the fragrance of the spices to infuse into the rice and cook very slowly over a low heat or low burning embers. The dough, known as purdah or veil, was used to seal the pot. Sometimes, a hot coal was placed on the top, which essentially created an oven so it cooked from the top down and the bottom up. Once the dish was cooked, the chef would tap the vessel and if it made a "dum" sound, the dish was ready. The seal would be opened, allowing the spices and aromatics to float out and invite all to come to dinner.

Talna (Frying)

This is the process of cooking food by immersing it in hot oil—both deep and shallow frying. Key points to remember are that the oil needs to be between 349°F and 375°F (176°C to 190°C) to fry effectively. If it's too cold, the food will soak up the oil and become greasy; if it's too hot, it will burn on the outside and be raw in the center. I was always taught to check the temperature by dropping in a little of the ingredient or batter—if it sinks to the bottom and floats to the top straightaway, it is ready.

Dhunaar (Smoke Seasoning)

This is a more unusual process that involves a quick smoking process using burning charcoal in a closed pot to infuse a smoky flavor. It can be used for meat dishes, dhals, and so on. I use this with some chutneys to give them a smoked flavor. It's easy to do in your kitchen using a foil tray or a makeshift tinfoil

tray. Heat coals over some flames on your cooker. Set the foil tray inside the pan you are wanting to smoke. Place the burning coals on the foil, add some whole spices, and pour over a tablespoon of ghee so it begins to smoke. Cover the pan and leave the smoke to infuse into the food for ten to fifteen minutes. It's a common method used in the desert areas of northern India, especially in the colder months.

Tawa Cooking (Griddle)

A tawa is a round, thin, concave cast-iron griddle pan. Helpful when very high temperatures are needed, it is mostly used in the home to cook unleavened breads, such as roti or paratha. On street corners in India, these huge griddles cook unique dishes that require fast cooking. The outside rim is used to keep the dishes warm as they are being sold. Snacks like pav bhaji and aloo tikki are typical tawa dishes. The veg masala is cooked in the center and constantly stirred to avoid burning. It's then smeared on bread rolls and sold. Other dishes include tawa chicken, tawa vegetables, and tawa paneer.

Galavat

Galavat refers to a method where softening agents like raw papaya paste (which contains papain), pineapple, mango, or yogurt are used to tenderize meat. In countries where the meat may be tougher or the type of meat requires more cooking (such as goat), these ingredients are very important. This method is slightly different from marinating because the process of marinating is more about penetrating the meat with other flavors, whereas this is solely about tenderizing. That said, you can also add other spices to infuse more flavor into the dish.

Loab/Rogan

Referring to the final stage of cooking, the oil used rises to the surface of the dish. It makes it look glossy and luxurious. This stage gives a dish that's been slowly cooked in a gravy its finished appearance.

1

Welcome Drinks & Snacks

Offering a little something to welcome your loved ones into your home is so important. Ideally, it should be warming and sweet, to grace the relationship you have. These recipes were chosen with that in mind, but they can double as great little bites for the kids, a lovely hostess gift to bring to a party, or something to share at work with colleagues. Like cookies, but a little more fun.

Coconut Ladoo

A ladoo (or ladu) is an Indian sweet, a flour, ghee, and sugar mixture that is cooked and shaped into spheres. There are many variations of ladoo; the most common uses gram flour, but you can also make them with semolina and add nuts, dried fruit, or coconut. Traditionally, they are given as gifts at weddings and religious festivals. This slightly less sweet version is made with coconut and cashews. If you are not a fan of cardamom, you can also flavor these with vanilla, cinnamon, rose water, or even rose petals.

Makes 10

1 teaspoon ghee

handful of cashews,
    roughly chopped

2 cups (150 g) grated coconut
    (fresh or desiccated)

1 cup (250 ml) milk

½ to ¾ cup (100 to 150 g) sugar

⅛ teaspoon green
    cardamom powder

shredded coconut to garnish

Heat ghee gently in a pan until it has melted, then add chopped cashews and roast until they turn golden. Remove from the pan (or they will burn) and leave to one side to cool.

In the same pan, add the coconut, milk, and sugar on medium heat. Stir together and cook until the mixture thickens and all the moisture completely evaporates. Remove from the heat.

Sprinkle in the cardamom powder and the toasted nuts, and stir to combine.

When the mixture is cool enough to handle, roll it into balls about the size of ping-pong balls.

Sprinkle the shredded coconut onto a plate and roll the balls in it to coat them.

Store them in an airtight container and refrigerate. You can also coat them in confectioners' sugar, chocolate powder, or nonpareils.

Top Tip • For a vegan version, just replace the milk with coconut or almond milk and the ghee with coconut oil.

Chai Financiers

If you're looking for something slightly more elevated, a financier is a small French almond cake baked in a rectangular mold that is flavored with a browned butter, or *beurre noisette*. They are crisp on the outside, super light, and moist. With its delicate flavoring, Chai has grown hugely popular in recent years; this infusion technique was shared with me by Sophie Uys, a very talented patisserie chef whom I have had the pleasure of working with.

Makes 12

3 tablespoons (45 g) unsalted butter

2 chai tea bags

6 to 7 tablespoons (45 g) ground almonds

5 to 6 tablespoons (45 g) plain flour

½ cup (90 g) caster sugar

2 egg whites, medium

icing and edible silverleaf, to decorate

Heat butter to melt, let it brown, and remove from the heat. Add the tea bags to infuse for 20 to 30 minutes.

Combine ground almonds, plain flour, and sugar.

Mix in egg whites and add in the warm butter.

Half fill the financier molds and bake at 350°F (180°C, or gas mark 4) for 12 to 15 minutes.

TO DECORATE

Spoon lines of the icing over one side of each financier and sprinkle with silver leaf.

Top Tip • This is a great recipe to try with different flavored tea bags—Earl Grey, turmeric chai, peppermint, and matcha are all great options.

Chocolate Barfi

This is essentially Indian fudge, but I've simplified the method and added chocolate (because everyone loves chocolate, right?). Barfi is usually made with milk and nuts, and flavored with cardamom, but you can also use nutmeg, rose water, or vanilla.

Makes 12-15

1½ cups (200 g) milk powder

approximately ¾ to 1 cup (200 ml) double cream or heavy cream

3½ tablespoons (50 g) unsalted butter

10 cardamom pods, ground, or ½ teaspoon cardamom powder

2¾ cups (517 g) sweetened condensed milk

1 cup (120 g) cocoa powder

2 tablespoons (16 g) pistachios, roughly crushed (optional)

Line a flat dish with parchment paper.

In a bowl, sieve in the milk powder and mix with the cream to make a lumpy dough. Set aside.

Heat the butter in a nonstick saucepan and add the cardamom powder.

Stir with the heat on low, and add the condensed milk and cocoa powder.

Once the cocoa powder has melted, add the cream and milk powder mixture. Stir to melt away any lumps.

Keep stirring until the mixture starts to leave the sides of the pan. Once this happens, pour it onto the flat dish and spread it with the back of a spoon so it's about 2 to 4 inches (5 to 10 cm) deep. I like to top with crushed pistachios.

Cool and set in the refrigerator for 2 to 3 hours or overnight.

Cut into squares and serve.

Ajwain & Kalonji Chips

In my world, savory snacks go hand in hand with sweet tea. We always had a packet of spicy Bombay mix in the cupboard in case any unexpected guest popped round (I loved picking out all the salty roasted peanuts before anyone else got a chance)! These chips are halfway between a crisp and a biscuit; they are crunchy, flaky, savory, salty, and oh-so-addictive—you won't be able to keep your hands off them.

Makes 20-25

1¼ cups (150 g) plain flour
2 tablespoons semolina flour
1 teaspoon salt
½ teaspoon ajwain/carom seeds
½ teaspoon kalonji seeds
¼ teaspoon baking powder
1 tablespoon (15 ml) oil
small amount of water
oil for frying

Put the flours, spices, baking powder, and oil into a wide bowl and start to rub together.

Add a little water and continue to mix until you get a firm dough. Let it rest for 20 to 30 minutes.

When you are ready to cook, begin to heat the oil for deep-frying on a gentle heat.

Take a ball of dough and roll it out until it's about ¹⁄₂₀ inch (1 mm) thick.

With a sharp knife, cut it into strips about 2 inches (5 cm) apart and then diagonally so each chip is about 4 inches (10 cm) long.

Test that the oil is hot enough by dropping in one chip; it should sink, sizzle, and rise. Once it turns golden and crispy, it's ready.

Fry the remaining chips in batches, remove, and drain on paper towels.

Fennel Masala Chai

Indian tea is an art—I was always teased as a kid that my tea was horrible, and I will still choose my aunts' over mine. It's a far cry from adding hot water to a tea bag—you have to allow the spices to infuse into the water, simmer, add the loose tea leaves, simmer, add the milk, bring to a boil without it boiling over (which I did all the time), and simmer again. This will give you 2 cups of tea.

Makes 4 cups

3 cups (710 ml) water
1 teaspoon fennel seeds
3 cardamom pods
2 cloves
¾-inch (2 cm) gingerroot, (optional)
1 tablespoon tea leaves or 2 tea bags
2 teaspoons sugar (or to taste)
approximately ½ cup (100 ml) milk

Place water in a small pan.

Add the fennel seeds, cardamom, and cloves (and ginger if making ginger tea) and heat the water.

Bring to the boil and leave for 2 to 3 minutes so the spices infuse into the water.

Add the tea and sugar. Reduce the heat and simmer for 2 to 3 minutes.

Pour in the milk (the tea should be a light caramel color). Turn the heat up and bring back to a boil. Just before it boils, reduce the heat and simmer for about 5 minutes to intensify. (Be careful, because it can boil over very quickly.)

Remove from the heat and strain the tea into small glasses.

Shakkar Para

One taste that transcends all cultures and countries: fried dough rolled in sugar. As children, we would ravage these—usually at the temple, on special occasions, or at weddings. For you, they might recall the county fair, or zeppoles on St. Joseph's Day. Delicious, no matter where!

Makes 20-25

2 cups (260 g) plain flour

4 to 5 tablespoons (60 to 75 ml) vegetable oil

around 4 tablespoons (60 ml) water to knead the dough

SUGAR SYRUP

2 cups (400 g) granulated white sugar

1 cup (250 ml) water

oil for frying

Place the flour in a large bowl and pour in the oil.

Rub the oil into the flour using your fingers until it's fully incorporated.

Start pouring in the water a little at a time until the dough just comes together. It should be fairly stiff, so don't add too much water. Leave it to rest for 15 to 20 minutes.

In a large pan, add the sugar and water and place on high heat, stirring until the sugar melts. Let it simmer to thicken for another 2 to 3 minutes, and set to one side.

Divide the dough into four pieces and then roll each one out to a thickness of ¼ inch (½ cm).

With a sharp knife slice strips about 1 inch (3 cm) long and then at an angle cut the other way to get diamonds (or any shape you like). These need to be fairly thick so they puff up and don't turn into crisps.

Heat the oil in a pan on medium heat. To check it's hot enough, add a little of the dough—it should sink and rise gently to the top. If it comes up too quickly, the oil is too hot, so let it cool a little.

Fry a few of the pastry diamonds until they turn light and golden, which should take about 7 to 8 minutes. Remove from the oil and drain on some paper towels.

While they are draining, heat the sugar syrup again. Place the cooked pastry puffs in the sugar syrup and stir on medium heat, then take off the heat.

The syrup will continue to thicken so you will need to stir every few minutes. The sugar crystallizes in around 7 to 8 minutes and starts coating the khurma (fried flour). Stir every few minutes until they are well coated and have absorbed the syrup.

Once cooled, they can be stored in an airtight container and should keep for 1 to 2 weeks.

Salted Lassi

A traditional lassi is essentially the leftover buttermilk that comes from the butter-making process. It's a good way to replenish the salt and electrolytes that your body loses in the heat. It's also incredibly thirst quenching. Since most people don't make butter at home these days, here is a quick version using yogurt instead.

Makes 2 glasses

2 cups (500 g) Greek yogurt
1 cup (250 ml) cold water
1 teaspoon roasted cumin seeds
1 teaspoon black salt
ice cubes
mint leaves to garnish

Put the yogurt into a tall jug and add the cold water.

Roast the cumin seeds in a pan and grind to a powder with a mortar and pestle.

Add half the salt and the roasted cumin powder to the yogurt mixture.

Blend everything together with a whisk until it is smooth. Check the seasoning and add a little more salt if required.

Put the ice cubes into glasses and pour the lassi in, adding a couple of mint leaves to the glasses.

Top Tip • If you prefer it sweet, then blitz some fruit (mango, strawberries, melon) with the yogurt, add a little sugar to taste, and pour over ice (you can also add a shot of rum to make it dirty)!

Aam Panna

Green mango water is another sweet and salty favorite designed to replace all that energy we lose in the heat.

Makes 2 glasses

1 pound (500 g) green mangoes

1 cup (30 g) mint leaves

1 cup (200 g) granulated sugar

2 teaspoons cumin seeds, roasted and ground

4 teaspoons black salt

6 cups (1½ l) water

Wash the green mangoes and place in a pressure cooker.

Cover with water and cook in the pressure cooker on high for 5 minutes.

Leave to cool, and then squeeze the flesh into a blender, discarding the skin and stones.

Add mint leaves, sugar, roasted cumin powder, and black salt to the blender and blend until smooth. (This is the concentrate that you can store in the fridge.)

Transfer the mango mixture to a large bowl or a pitcher. Add water and stir well.

Refrigerate the panna for a few hours and serve chilled over ice.

Note: You can keep it refrigerated for 3 to 4 days.

Top Tip • Use fizzy water to turn this into a carbonated drink.

Nimbu Pani

This is Indian lemonade that's sweet, sour, spicy, and tangy. So refreshing you can't help but try it.

Makes 2 glasses

3 cups (710 ml) water

2 lemons or 3 limes

1 tablespoon (13 g) sugar
(may need to add more)

1 teaspoon black salt or rock salt

1 teaspoon cumin powder

½ teaspoon chaat masala

4 to 5 mint leaves

a few ice cubes

lemon slices (optional)

Put the water in a jug.

Slice the lemons or limes and squeeze the juice into the jug, discarding any seeds.

Add sugar, black salt, cumin powder, chaat masala, mint leaves, and ice cubes.

Mix it all until the sugar dissolves and check the seasoning, adjusting if desired.

Pour into tall glasses and add lemon slices, if using. Serve chilled.

2

Feisty Finger Foods

Did you know that traditionally, Indian food is always consumed with your fingers? It has nothing to do with lack of cutlery or utensils—it's more about the holistic and spiritual approach Indians take to their food.

Schmokin' Tandoori Wings

Wings are the best type of finger food, because one wing is never enough! The zingy lime, fresh coriander, red chilli, and red onion slices sprinkled over the top add a tangy salad flavor, that complements that which has been imparted from the marinade.

Makes 12-15

2¼ pounds (1 kg) chicken wings
    split into drumettes and flats
¾ cup (200 g) Greek yogurt
4 garlic cloves, crushed
2 teaspoons fresh ginger, grated
juice from 1 lemon
1 tablespoon garam masala
2 teaspoons Kashmiri chilli powder
1 teaspoon cumin seeds, crushed
1 teaspoon salt
1 tablespoon dried fenugreek
    leaves (kasoori methi)
1 tablespoon gram flour
1 tablespoon (15 ml) mustard oil

TO SERVE
fresh lime wedges
fresh coriander, chopped
red chillies, sliced (optional)
red onion, sliced

Preheat the oven to 400°F (204°C, or gas mark 6).

Combine all the marinade ingredients together and stir.

Place the chicken wings in the bowl, and coat them fully with the marinade. Allow to marinate for at least 30 minutes (but you can leave them for up to 24 hours covered in the fridge).

Preheat the grill for 15 minutes. Place the chicken wings on the grill and cook for 20 to 25 minutes, or until the chicken is cooked through and caramelized all over.

To cook in the oven, line a tray with foil. Place a rack over the foil and put the wings on the rack.

Cook for 25 to 30 minutes on one side, turn, and cook for another 15 minutes on the other side to ensure they are crisp all over.

To serve the wings, squeeze on fresh lime juice and sprinkle with the coriander, chillies, and onions.

Top Tips • To add smoky flavor, I use the smoke seasoning technique discussed in the Introduction (see Dhunaar, page 14). All you need to do is remove the wings from the oven and place a piece of charcoal on the flame until it starts to get hot. Place the hot charcoal into an old ramekin or on some aluminum foil in the tray of wings.

Put 2 green cardamom pods, 2 cloves, and a bay leaf in the ramekin around the hot charcoal, and pour a heaped teaspoon of ghee over the charcoal. This will start to smoke very quickly. Cover the tray of wings with foil for 3 to 4 minutes so they take on the smoky flavor.

Hariyali Chicken Tikka Skewers

Tikka, or tikki, just means small, bite-size pieces. Hariyali is a green marinade, but you can also make this dish with a tandoori marinade. The Hariyali marinade uses mint, coriander, and spinach, with some very subtle spices in a yogurt base. I like to use peppers here as well, because it makes the whole dish colorful, and we all know that eating the rainbow is not only fun but good for us too. These skewers are great with rice or a salad, and kids love them in wraps (but you might have to pick out the peppers).

Serves 4

MARINADE

1 teaspoon cumin seeds

1 teaspoon coriander seeds

1 bunch fresh coriander, leaves and stems (more to serve)

½ bunch fresh mint leaves

handful of fresh spinach

4 garlic cloves, minced

1-inch (3 cm) piece of fresh ginger

4 fresh green chillies

juice from 1 lemon (more to serve)

1 teaspoon salt

1 teaspoon garam masala

1 teaspoon Kashmiri chilli powder

1 tablespoon (15 ml) mustard oil

3 tablespoons (45 g) Greek yogurt

5 to 6 boneless chicken thighs or 4 boneless chicken breasts, cut into chunks

1 red pepper, cut into chunks

1 yellow pepper, cut into chunks

2 red onions, cut into chunks

Put the cumin and coriander seeds into a pan and toast them until they are fragrant. Crush roughly with a mortar and pestle leave to cool.

Put the coriander, fresh mint, spinach, garlic, ginger, chillies, lemon juice, salt, garam masala, chilli powder, and oil into a blender, and blitz to a smooth paste.

Empty this paste into a bowl, and mix in the yogurt and crushed cumin and coriander seeds.

Combine the chicken, peppers, and onions with the marinade and let it sit for at least 30 minutes (even better if you have more time).

Heat the oven to 400°F (200°C, or gas mark 6). Thread the chicken, peppers, and onions onto six metal or wooden skewers. (If using wooden skewers, soak them in cold water for about 20 minutes before using.)

Cook on a wire rack in the oven for 25 minutes, or on a grill for about 10 to 15 minutes, until cooked through, turning occasionally.

Garnish with coriander and a good squeeze of lemon juice to serve.

Chicken Momos

Momos are India's answer to the dumpling, inspired by Tibetan dumplings. There is a strong Nepalese influence in Indian cuisine, and this Nepali street food can be found on many Indian street corners. Filled with meat or vegetables, momos are usually flavored with spring onions, fresh coriander, ginger, garlic, chillies, and a few fragrant spices. They are pretty versatile, so you can use minced chicken, pork, lamb, vegetables, or even paneer. Traditionally these are steamed, but you can also pan fry them for a crispy finish.

I have also included a classic momo tomato achaar in the recipe below, but if you prefer, some crispy chilli oil is just as good.

Makes 12-15

MOMO FILLING

4 to 5 spring or green onions

4 garlic cloves

1 to 2 green chillies

2-inch (5 cm) piece of ginger

1 pound (500 g) ground chicken

1 teaspoon turmeric

1 teaspoon salt or soy sauce

1 teaspoon Kashmiri chilli powder

1 teaspoon coriander seeds, crushed

1 teaspoon cumin seeds, crushed

1 to 2 tablespoons (15 to 30 ml) vegetable oil

handful of fresh coriander leaves

MOMO WRAPPERS

2½ cups (300 g) plain flour

pinch of salt

water

MOMO ACHAAR

approximately ¾ to 1 cup (200 ml) water

3 large ripe tomatoes, diced

4 to 5 dried Kashmiri chillies

4 garlic cloves

1 tablespoon fresh ginger, grated

1 tablespoon (13 g) sugar

1 tablespoon (15 ml) vinegar

¼ teaspoon salt

1 tablespoon (15 ml) soy sauce

MOMO FILLING

Mince the onions with the garlic. Heat a tablespoon of oil in a pan and add the onion mixture; sauté for a few minutes on medium heat.

Mince the ginger and green chillies and add to the pan. Leave to cool for a minute.

Add the mixture to the ground chicken, then add the turmeric, salt (or soy sauce), chilli powder, coriander, and crushed cumin, and mix everything into the meat.

Add 1 to 2 tablespoons of vegetable oil and mix it again. This keeps the mixture nice and juicy.

Add some finely chopped coriander, and mix it all together.

MOMO WRAPPERS

Put the flour and a pinch of salt into a bowl.

Add water, a little at a time, to the flour and stir to make the dough.

Knead the dough for a few more minutes until it is soft and pliable. Let it rest for 20 minutes. Divide the dough into 20 equal pieces.

With a rolling pin, roll the dough as thin as possible into circles. You can also roll it out so it's about 1 mm thick and use a cutter to cut out circles approximately 3 inches (7 to 8 cm) in diameter.

MAKE THE MOMOS

Put roughly 1 tablespoon of the filling into the center of each wrapper.

Pleat the edges of the wrapper and rotate until it's pleated and sealed all the way around.

Oil the bottom of your steamer to keep the momos from sticking, and place the momos into the steamer so they are not touching each other.

Steam for 20 to 25 minutes, until the outside is no longer sticky.

Top Tip • Vegetarian Momos
You can use vegetables of your choice, paneer, or any meat-free product. Just finely grate or chop, and sauté with the onion and garlic mixture to soften the vegetables rather than adding them raw. If it's your first time, try cabbage, pea, and paneer for a simple and delicious momo!

TO PAN FRY

Add a tablespoon of oil to a sauté pan over medium heat. Add the momos, and once they start to brown, add about ¼ to ½ cup (50 to 100 ml) of water and put the lid on the pan. Let them steam for 10 minutes. (You may need to reduce the heat.)

Remove the lid, and allow the water to evaporate.

Toss the momos in soy sauce and chilli sauce, or in the achaar (recipe to follow).

Momos are great on their own, but sauce takes the taste one step further. In fact, some of the most popular momo shops in Nepal owe it to their unique achaar.

MOMO ACHAAR

Heat approximately ¾ to 1 cup (200 ml) of water in a pan and add the diced tomatoes, dried red chillies, garlic cloves, and 1 tablespoon grated ginger, and boil for 10 to 15 minutes until you have a pulp and the garlic is soft.

Pour everything into a blender with sugar, vinegar, salt, and soy sauce and blitz until smooth. Check seasoning, and serve with the momos.

Lamb Kebabs

Traditionally, kebabs are cooked on long metal skewers in the tandoor oven, but this is my very quick version to cook at home, as a starter or a quick snack. Packed full of flavor, they will always get gobbled up! If you are worried about the spice level, just leave the chillies out.

I am a real advocate for getting the kids cooking, and these lamb kebabs were the first thing my daughter learned to cook all by herself at five years old. They are still her favorite! These kebabs are delicious served with the mint chutney on page 142.

Makes 8

1 pound (500 g) minced lamb

1 medium onion, very finely diced

4 garlic cloves, very finely chopped

1 tablespoon fresh ginger, grated

1 teaspoon salt

1 to 2 green chillies, finely chopped

½ teaspoon red chilli powder (optional)

2 teaspoons cumin seeds, crushed

2 teaspoons garam masala

1 teaspoon dried fenugreek leaves (kasoori methi)

handful coriander, finely chopped

1 teaspoon oil in a small dish

1 red chilli, finely sliced to garnish

Heat the oven to 350°F (180°C, or gas mark 4), line an oven tray with foil, and place a wire rack in the tray.

Place the minced lamb in a large bowl, add all the other ingredients (except the oil and red chilli slices), and mix together using your hands to ensure all the spices are evenly distributed.

Wash hands and rub them with a little oil to help shape the kebabs.

Take a small amount of the mixture and shape it into a small kebab about 4 inches (10 cm) long and 1 inch (3 cm) thick. (Keep them fairly thick, so they stay moist and delicious.)

Place the kebabs on the rack and place the tray in the oven. Cook the kebabs for 15 minutes, remove and turn them, and cook for an additional 10 to 15 minutes. You can leave them for another 5 minutes to brown and crisp up a little.

For an appetizer, serve with crisp salad leaves and thinly sliced onions, with a side of tangy mint chutney. For a snack, stuff in a warmed pita with salad, mint chutney, and a dollop of yogurt.

Top Tip • These are just as good with beef, pork, or chicken. For some added love, with pork, add 1 teaspoon crushed fennel seeds; with chicken, add finely diced green and red peppers. With beef, add 1 teaspoon paprika.

Amritsari Fish Bites

I call these fish fingers with a *pow*! I learned my love for a fish finger sandwich from my dad—his was the best. Whether a frozen fish finger from the supermarket or one of these pakora bites, it has a special place in my heart. The marinade gives the fish a wonderful tang, and the silky gram flour batter is spiked with chillies and carom seeds. Once fried, these are super crispy, and perfect to dip into tomato ketchup as a little snack, in a taco with salad and slaw, or on a bun as a fishwich. I always go for a meaty white fish, but salmon works just as well. The chickpea flour is a great gluten-free alternative to standard breading.

Makes 15-20

14 ounces (400 g) white fish loin,
    cut into large chunks

MARINADE
juice from ½ lime or lemon
1 tablespoon fresh ginger, grated
2 garlic cloves, pounded
1 teaspoon garam masala
½ teaspoon salt
½ teaspoon turmeric
1 chilli, finely chopped (optional)

BATTER
¾ cup (100 g) gram flour, sieved
1 teaspoon carom seeds or
    cumin seeds
handful coriander, chopped
1 teaspoon baking powder
1 teaspoon chilli powder
½ teaspoon salt

water
rapeseed oil for frying

Remove moisture from the fish by drying on a paper towel.

Make a marinade paste by mixing the lime/lemon juice, ginger, garlic, garam masala, salt, turmeric, and chopped chilli. It should be a dry paste.

Rub the marinade all over the fish and refrigerate for at least 30 minutes (the longer, the better).

Sieve the gram flour into a separate bowl and add carom seeds, coriander, baking powder, chilli powder, salt, and a little water to make a thick batter. Beat to aerate the mixture.

Heat the oil in a wok or karahi to a medium heat. (Note: If the oil is too hot, the batter will cook too quickly and the fish will remain uncooked.)

Dip one of the marinated fish pieces into the batter to cover, and very gently place in the hot oil. Leave to cook for about 3 minutes, using a slotted spoon to move the pakora around.

Once crisp and golden brown, remove and set on paper towels. Taste to check the seasoning, and adjust if required.

Continue to cook the rest in small batches.

Top Tip • To test if the oil is hot enough, drop a little batter into the oil—if it sinks and starts to sizzle and floats straight up to the surface, the oil is ready.

Garlic Chilli King Prawns

Prawns are widely loved because they are sweet, versatile, and so quick to cook. Always go for the freshest raw prawns you can find, but this recipe also works with frozen prawns. This is a super speedy dish that is perfect for sharing. Just as with Spanish tapas, you need bread to mop up the garlic and chilli sauce—soft, fluffy naan are perfect for this!

Serves 4

1 pound (500 g) shell-on king prawns

1 teaspoon coriander seeds, crushed

½ teaspoon cumin seeds, crushed

½ teaspoon turmeric

½ teaspoon Kashmiri chilli powder

½ teaspoon salt

MASALA

2 tablespoons (30 ml) oil

½ teaspoon brown mustard seeds

½ teaspoon cumin seeds

1 garlic clove, sliced

1 inch (3 cm) piece fresh ginger, julienned

1 chilli, sliced

juice from a lemon

½ teaspoon Kashmiri chilli powder

handful of fresh coriander leaves, chopped

Wash the prawns and pat dry with paper towels.

Sprinkle the crushed coriander and cumin seeds over the prawns with the turmeric, chilli powder, and salt, and mix well. Set to one side for 10 minutes.

Heat the oil in a wide-based pan and add the mustard and cumin seeds. Just as they sizzle, add the sliced garlic, ginger, and fresh chilli.

Quickly stir in the prawns, reduce the heat, and cook for about 2 to 3 minutes.

Squeeze in the lemon juice and add the chilli powder, and toss to coat the prawns. The oil and lemon will create a bit of a sauce.

Once the prawns have turned pink and cooked through (another minute or so), throw in the fresh chopped coriander to serve.

Serve with a lemon wedge and fluffy naan.

Aloo Pakora Crisps

Potato chips the Indian way—thin or thick slices of potato coated in a gram flour batter and fried to crispy golden discs. These bites are great to dunk into a tamarind chutney, but I also love to put a sprinkling of chaat masala over them for a spicy tang, and a little chilli powder for heat. My mum made these for the kids at every family gathering (leaving out the chillies). In between games of tag, we would surround the table, giggling and dunking them joyfully into tomato ketchup. There were never enough.

Serves 4

¾ cup (100 g) gram flour, sieved
1 tablespoon rice flour
salt, to taste
½ teaspoon carom seeds
1 teaspoon cumin seeds
1 tablespoon fresh ginger, grated
½ teaspoon red chilli powder
1 teaspoon garam masala powder
pinch of fresh coriander, chopped
⅔ to ¾ cup (156 to 177 ml) water
1 medium potato
1 teaspoon chaat masala powder
    for sprinkling

Mix the flours and spices with the water. Check the seasoning, adjusting if needed. This should be a lovely, thick batter.

Peel and thinly slice the potato into rounds, about 1 inch (3 cm) thick.

Heat the oil for frying in a kadai or large pan on medium heat. You can test the oil is hot enough by dropping in a little batter. If it sizzles and comes to the surface, the oil is ready.

Dip each potato slice in the batter and place it gently in the hot oil. Fry aloo pakoras until they are golden and crisp. They will take 3 to 4 minutes to cook through. If they brown too quickly on the outside, they won't cook through.

Remove from the oil with a slotted spoon and drain on paper towels to remove excess oil.

Repeat with the remaining aloo, cooking in batches.

Sprinkle over chaat masala powder and serve with a mint chutney.

Top Tip • **Make a lot!**

Kashmiri Spiced Halloumi

I love halloumi—who doesn't? But the saltiness of the cheese is just wonderful combined with the warming spices and the heat of the Kashmiri chilli powder in this one. This is great as a snack dipped in a tamarind chutney, on top of a salad (try it with watermelon), or even in a burger with all the trimmings.

Serves 4

4 garlic cloves, crushed

2-inch (5 cm) piece of fresh ginger, grated

1 green chilli, finely chopped

7 ounces (200 g) halloumi (or paneer or tofu), cut into 2-inch (5 cm) fingers

1 tablespoon (15 ml) mustard oil (or rapeseed oil)

juice of 1 large lemon

¾ cup (200 g) Greek yogurt

1 teaspoon salt

2 teaspoons garam masala

1 teaspoon cumin seeds, crushed

1 tablespoon Kashmiri red chilli powder

1 tablespoon dried fenugreek leaves (kasoori methi)

handful of fresh coriander leaves, chopped

1 lemon, chopped into wedges

Blend the garlic, ginger, and chilli with a mortar and pestle.

Place the halloumi fingers in a dish and stir in the blended ingredients along with the mustard oil and lemon juice.

In a separate dish, mix the remaining ingredients with the yogurt to create a paste.

Add this spiced yogurt paste to the halloumi. Cover and leave to marinade for at least 30 minutes (the longer, the better).

Heat the oven to 350°F (180°C, or gas mark 4).

Transfer to a lined oven tray and cook for about 10 to 15 minutes.

Sprinkle over the chopped coriander and serve with lemon wedges.

Top Tip • Alternatively, you can cut the halloumi into large cubes; marinate with mushrooms, peppers, and onions; and skewer onto bamboo skewers to cook as kebabs!

Nut & Lentil Kofta

No longer are lentils considered a poor man's protein—there are so many new and interesting ways to use them. Whether it's a basic dhal or a spiced fritter, they are a great source of flavor and texture—and easy to cook, too. I have added some basic vegetables to make these kofta bites fun and nutritious. I sometimes put this mixture into a loaf pan, press it down, and bake to make a nut roast, which is a great vegetarian option for Sunday lunch.

Makes 15-20

1 tablespoon (15 ml) ghee or oil

1 teaspoon cumin seeds

1 dried chilli

1 large onion, finely chopped

2 garlic cloves, finely chopped

1-inch (3 cm) piece of fresh ginger, grated

7 ounces (200 g) chestnut mushrooms, sliced

3½ ounces (100 g) paneer, grated

1 large carrot, grated

1 teaspoon Kashmiri chilli powder

½ teaspoon turmeric

2 tomatoes, chopped

1¼ cups (300 ml) water

3½ ounces (100 g) red lentils

3½ ounces (100 g) walnuts and cashews, roughly chopped

3½ ounces (100 g) mature cheddar cheese, grated

handful of fresh coriander, chopped

2 tablespoons gram flour, toasted in a dry pan

Preheat the oven to 350°F (180°C, or gas mark 4).

Line an oven tray with parchment paper.

Heat the ghee in a large frying pan on medium heat, and add the cumin seeds and dried chilli until sizzling and fragrant.

Add the onion and cook for about 5 minutes, until soft.

Add the garlic and ginger, and stir for a few minutes.

Add the sliced mushrooms and cook until they soften; then stir in the paneer and grated carrot. Cook the mixture for about 3 minutes, and then add the chilli powder and turmeric, cooking for just a minute.

Add the tomatoes and cook for about 1 minute until they start to break down, then add the water and season with salt.

Stir in the lentils and bring to a boil; reduce heat. Leave to simmer over a very gentle heat until all the liquid has been absorbed and the mixture is fairly dry (about 10 minutes). Set aside to cool.

Stir in the roughly chopped nuts with the cheese and coriander. If it feels wet, sprinkle in the toasted gram flour.

Once mixed through, coat your hand in a little oil and make balls the size of golf balls. Place on the oven tray.

Bake for 20 minutes on one side. Turn them and bake for an additional 10 minutes until they are firm when gently pressed.

Serve with a mint chutney.

Top Tip • Gram flour works to thicken, but it's really important to toast the flour in a dry pan first. It will start to release a sweet aroma once it is toasted. Remove to a bowl to cool or it will burn. To make this recipe vegan, simply replace the ghee with coconut oil and omit the cheese and paneer. It's a good idea to add a tablespoon of a tangy Mango Chutney (page 145) or Indian Tomato Ketchup (page 143) to help bind it.

Feisty Finger Foods

Vegetable Samosa

One of India's most famous items is the samosa, and I love how slightly different versions can be found across the globe: In South Africa, it's the samoosa; in Somalia, it's the sambuus; in Iran, it's the sambosa. Whatever you call it, it's a wonderful crisp triangular pastry parcel filled with a spiced mixture. In India, it's usually potato and peas, but you can use a filling of minced lamb, beetroot, and coconut, or even spicy chickpeas. The pastry also varies—some prefer a crisp phyllo style (which you can buy), though I personally find the Punjabi style below much more satisfying.

Makes 15–20

FILLING

4 potatoes

1 teaspoon rapeseed oil

½ teaspoon cumin seeds

⅓ cup (70 g) frozen peas

1 tablespoon grated ginger

1 teaspoon salt

2 chillies, finely chopped

½ teaspoon chilli powder

1 to 2 teaspoons garam masala

2 tablespoons fresh coriander, chopped

PASTE

1 tablespoon plain flour in a small bowl

splash of cold water

PASTRY

1½ cups (200 g) plain flour

1½ tablespoons rapeseed oil

pinch of salt

approximately ½ cup (100 ml) water

vegetable oil for frying

FILLING

Gently boil the potatoes with the skin on (do not boil too vigorously) for about 25 minutes until soft. Remove from the heat and allow to cool. Once cooled, peel the skin off with your fingers.

Cut the potatoes into small ½-inch (1 cm) cubes and place in a large bowl.

In a small frying pan, heat the oil and fry the cumin seeds. When sizzling, carefully add the peas and gently fry for a few minutes to soften. Remove from the heat and cool before adding to the potatoes.

Add the grated ginger, salt, chillies, chilli powder, garam masala, and fresh coriander to the potatoes and stir. Adjust the seasoning, if desired, and refrigerate for 10 minutes.

PASTE

Create flour glue by adding water to the flour to make a thick, sticky paste.

PASTRY

Place flour, oil, and salt in a bowl and rub the mixture together.

With your hand, sprinkle in a little water at a time to bring the dough together.

Continue to add the water in this way until the dough forms. Using wet hands, knead the dough until it is soft and no longer sticking to your hands or the bowl.

Refrigerate for 10 minutes. Heat up a tawa (Indian griddle pan) or frying pan on the lowest heat setting.

Take a small tangerine-sized ball of the dough and roll it between your palms to make a smooth ball. Flatten and roll out with a rolling pin to create a thin, round disc the size of a side plate, flouring when necessary. Place the disc on the tawa for 4 seconds. Remove and place on a chopping board. Using a sharp knife, slice the disc in half so you are left with two semicircles.

MAKE THE SAMOSA

Place one semicircle on your hand with the flat edge at the top and the cooked side facing you. Dip your finger in the flour paste and spread it across the straight edge.

Fold in the two corners so they meet in the middle ensuring one edge overlaps the other and press together to seal all the way down to create a smooth upside-down cone.

Turn the cone over so the pointed end is at the bottom. Using a spoon, fill the cone with the potato filling to two-thirds of the way up.

Seal the opening with the paste, creating a triangle pastry. Place it on the tray and pat down to even the filling out. Repeat with the remaining dough until you use up all the filling.

COOK THE SAMOSA

Heat the oil for deep-frying in a large pan. You can test whether it's hot enough by dropping in a little bit of pastry—if it bubbles and floats to the top immediately, the oil is ready.

Very carefully slip one samosa into the hot oil and leave to cook for a few seconds. As the pastry begins to bubble, turn it over using a slotted spoon.

Gently cook until it turns a beautiful golden brown. Remove from the oil and place on paper towels. As you become more confident, fry two or three samosas at the same time.

3

Sharing Platters

Large plates and sharing platters make dining an interactive experience, which is definitely my kind of dining. It's also a great way to serve larger groups of people without exhausting yourself! They say you eat with your eyes first, so these dishes are all about color, vibrancy, and beautiful aromas—with lots of sides like pickles, dips, and kachumber salads—to give you a soul-satisfying experience.

Jeera Aloo Wedges

Cumin seeds, when used whole, add a nutty texture that works so well on these potato wedges. These chunky-cut wedges are coated in a simple selection of spices and baked until crisp. They come out with a nutty, warming crunch that works as both a lovely side for your burger or for dipping into a cucumber raita as part of a sharing board.

Serves 4

4 large potatoes (Maris Piper or russet work well)

1 tablespoon (15 ml) oil

1 teaspoon salt

2 teaspoons cumin seeds

2 teaspoons Kashmiri chilli powder

1 teaspoon garam masala

1 teaspoon garlic powder

Preheat the oven to 350°F (180°C, or gas mark 4).

Wash and scrub the potatoes; then cut into chunky wedges with the skin left on.

In a large, roomy bowl, combine all the spices and oil to make a rub. Add the potatoes and mix, using your hands to coat them with the oil rub.

Place wedges on an oven tray skin side down.

Place in the oven to cook for 25 to 30 minutes until crisp.

Top Tip • To turn these into loaded potato skins and make them even more special, just sprinkle over some grated Parmesan and cheddar cheese with two chopped spring or green onions (add a chopped red chili too). Dip them into the Pomegranate Raita (page 148) or Indian Tomato Ketchup (page 143).

Chilli Cheese Bites

These are such a fun and delicious snack to make! If you are making them for kids who are sensitive to spice, just leave the chilli out. There are many other options for flavoring, including using ground fennel and cumin seeds and serving with a mint chutney.

Makes 12-15

1 large potato, boiled and grated

7 ounces (200 g) paneer, grated

2 ounces (55 g) cheddar cheese, grated

4 tablespoons (30 g) corn flour

large pinch of fresh coriander, chopped

1 teaspoon garam masala

½ teaspoon salt

2 red chillies, finely chopped

1 tablespoon fresh ginger, grated

1.75 ounces (50 g) mozzarella cheese, cut into small cubes

3 tablespoons (23 g) plain flour

3 tablespoons (44 ml) water

½ cup (60 g) bread crumbs

oil for frying

Mix the boiled potato, paneer, cheddar cheese, corn flour, coriander, garam masala, salt, chopped red chillies, and ginger in a bowl.

Make small balls from the mixture.

Flatten each ball and put a cube of mozzarella in the center.

Now roll the potato coating together to cover the cheese and repeat with all the balls.

In another bowl, add plain flour and water to make a thin paste. In a third bowl, add the bread crumbs.

Dip each ball into the flour paste, and then roll them in the bread crumbs until completely coated. Refrigerate the balls to firm them up until you are ready to cook them.

When you are ready to cook, heat the oil in a deep fryer to about 350°F (180°C) and deep-fry the balls until golden and crisp. Remove and place on paper towels.

Curried Jackfruit Tacos

The tropical jackfruit tree is native to southwest India. It bears big, green fruit, which turns yellow as it ripens. Its flesh, seeds, and pods are all edible, and, when ripe, its distinctive flavor is usually described as a cross between a banana and a pineapple. The raw, or green, jackfruit is a standard ingredient in the Indian kitchen that has become very popular with the rise in vegan cuisine. Its fibrous, meaty texture and ability to absorb other flavors make it a fantastic alternative to meat. It also has a sharp tang, so dishes with barbecue or curry flavors work well. You can buy it fresh or canned, and for this recipe you can use either.

Makes 10-12

1 teaspoon oil
1 teaspoon cumin seeds
1 teaspoon mustard seeds
1 teaspoon kalonji seeds
2 bay leaves
2 dried Kashmiri red chillies
1 small onion, sliced
5 garlic cloves, sliced
2 medium tomatoes, finely chopped
1-inch (3 cm) piece ginger, sliced
1 teaspoon coriander seeds, crushed
1 green chilli, chopped
½ teaspoon turmeric
¼ teaspoon black pepper
½ teaspoon salt or to taste
2 14-ounce (400 g) cans green jackfruit, drained and rinsed
1 cup (250 ml) water
1 teaspoon garam masala
handful of fresh coriander, chopped

15 taco shells (see recipe below)

Heat the oil in a pan over medium heat and add the cumin and mustard seeds. When they sizzle and become aromatic, add the kalonji seeds.

Add the bay leaves and red chillies and stir in the onion. Sauté for 5 to 6 minutes before adding the garlic. Stir until the onions turn a golden color.

Stir in the chopped tomatoes, ginger, crushed coriander seeds, chopped chilli, turmeric, black pepper, and salt. Mix well.

When the tomatoes start to break down, add the rinsed jackfruit, mixing to coat with the masala. Cover the pan and cook for 15 to 20 minutes.

Add water, cover, and cook for 15 more minutes before tasting. Check the seasoning and adjust if required. Leave the lid off the pan and let it reduce to thicken a little. Remove from the heat.

Using two forks, shred the jackfruit. Sprinkle with the garam masala and chopped coriander.

Serve with crispy lettuce and a dollop of yogurt inside the taco shells.

HOMEMADE TACO SHELLS

Mix 2 cups (252 g) of corn flour with 1 teaspoon salt.

Gradually add hot water, up to about 1½ cups (350 ml). But only add what you need to make a dough, kneading until smooth. Let it sit for 30 minutes.

Preheat the oven to 375°F (190°C, or gas mark 5). Make the dough into about fifteen balls and roll out or use a tortilla press to flatten them. To get them round, use a side plate as a template, cutting around it.

Prick each taco all over with a fork and place on a warm griddle, turning over after 2 to 3 minutes, and then hang the taco over two bars on your oven rack and bake for 8 to 10 minutes until crisp.

Watermelon & Feta Chaat

A chaat is a sort of blend between a refreshing salad and a tangy salsa. A basic chaat is about stimulating all the tastebuds in the mouth, so it contains sweet, sour, bitter, and umami flavors. And it's also about texture: soft, smooth, creamy, and crispy. That may sound like a tall order, but this one is pretty easy to pull together, and perfect for a summer gathering. Plus watermelon and feta makes an incredible combination.

Serves 4

PAAPRI CRISPS

2 cups (250 g) atta (wheat flour)

½ teaspoon baking powder

pinch of salt

1 teaspoon carom seeds

3 tablespoons (45 ml) rapeseed oil or ghee

¼ cup (60 ml) water

GREEN CHUTNEY

handful of coriander leaves

handful of mint leaves

1 green chilli

2-inch (5 cm) piece of ginger

½ teaspoon black rock salt

salt, to taste

½ teaspoon garam masala

juice of 1 lemon

SWEET DATE AND TAMARIND CHUTNEY

3 ounces (85 g) seedless tamarind

½ cup (80 g) seedless dates

2 cups (450 ml) water

¼ cup (40 g) grated jaggery (or brown sugar)

½ teaspoon coriander seeds, crushed

½ teaspoon cumin seeds, crushed

½ teaspoon dry ginger powder

½ teaspoon red chilli powder

1 teaspoon black salt or rock salt

PAAPRI

Add the flour and baking powder to a bowl and mix in the salt and carom seeds.

Add the oil and start to knead to form a dough, pouring in the water a little at a time until you have a soft dough. If it's sticky, add a little more flour. Let it rest for 15 minutes. Knead a little more to soften.

Preheat the oven to 400°F (200°C, or gas mark 6).

Take a ball and roll out to make a roti about 1⁄16 inch (2 to 3 mm) thick.

With a fork, make holes all over the surface of the rolled-out roti.

Using a cookie cutter, cut out round discs and place onto a baking sheet lined with parchment paper.

Bake in the oven for 8 to 10 minutes, turning halfway, just until they turn golden (keep an eye on them).

Remove from the oven and leave to cool until crisp.

GREEN CHUTNEY

Place all the ingredients into a blender and blitz to make a chutney. Add a little water if required.

SWEET DATE AND TAMARIND CHUTNEY

Put the tamarind, dates, and water into a pan and cook for about 10 minutes on a gentle heat.

Add the jaggery and stir, and let it come to a boil. Once the jaggery has dissolved, the mixture will start to thicken.

Stir in all the spices and salt, and simmer for about 20 to 25 minutes. Remove the pan from the heat and cool.

Sieve the chutney mixture into a blender and grind until the chutney is smooth. Add a little water if required. After using, store in a clean jar in the refrigerator for up to 3 weeks.

SPICED WATERMELON

half a watermelon, cubed

7 ounces (200 g) block feta cheese, cubed

1 green chilli, finely chopped

handful of mint leaves, sliced

1 small red onion, finely diced

2 tablespoons chopped coriander leaves

1 teaspoon roasted cumin powder

2 teaspoons chaat masala powder

¼ teaspoon red chilli powder (optional)

1 teaspoon black salt

handful of crispy puffed rice and sev (crunchy noodles)

SPICED WATERMELON

Place all the ingredients in a bowl and stir. Taste and adjust the seasoning if necessary.

TO SERVE

Plate individual paapri crisps and pile on the watermelon and feta mix.

Top with a blob of green chutney and a blob of sweet date and tamarind chutney.

Sprinkle a little of the puffed rice on top.

Top Tip • This chaat is all about vibrant summer flavors, hence the watermelon and feta, but if you fancy something more authentically Indian, just use canned chickpeas and some boiled, diced potatoes instead!

Sharing Platters

Spiced Sausage Rolls

There is something super satisfying about sausage rolls, both making them and eating them. Plus, everyone loves them. Get creative with the filling—add a spicy kick, cheese, dried fruit, crushed nuts, chorizo, or even lentils, and to make it easy, use ready-made puff pastry.

Makes 15-20

SPICED PORK FILLING

1 tablespoon (15 ml) rapeseed oil

1 teaspoon cumin seeds

1 medium onion, very finely diced

1 tablespoon fresh ginger, grated

2 garlic cloves, minced

1 green chilli, finely chopped

2 pounds (800 g) ground pork

1 teaspoon salt

1 teaspoon chilli powder (optional)

large pinch fresh coriander leaves, chopped

1 teaspoon garam masala

PASTRY

1 pound (500 g) block of ready-made puff pastry

OR

6 ounces (175 g) unsalted butter, chilled and cut into small cubes separated into 4 equal amounts

2¾ cups (350 g) plain flour

pinch of salt

3 to 4 tablespoons (45 to 60 ml) iced water

TURMERIC EGG WASH

1 egg, beaten

splash of milk

½ teaspoon turmeric

kalonji seeds to garnish

SPICED PORK FILLING

Heat the oil in a pan and sauté the cumin seeds. Then add the diced onion, grated ginger, minced garlic, and chilli, and cook until soft. Leave to cool.

Mix the onion mixture with the minced pork, salt, chilli powder, chopped coriander leaves, and garam masala, and set to one side.

PASTRY

If not using ready-made puff pastry, combine a quarter of the butter cubes in a bowl with the flour and salt, then add just enough cold water to bring together to make a firm dough.

Dust your surface with flour and roll out the dough to make a rectangle about ⅓ inch (1 cm) thick. Dot another quarter of the butter over the rolled pastry. Fold the two short ends into the middle so they overlap. Turn the pastry by 45 degrees and roll out again and repeat the process with the remaining butter. You need to do this to get air and butter into the pastry layers so the pastry expands during cooking and puffs. Turn the pastry by 45 degrees and repeat the process four or five more times.

Wrap the pastry in plastic wrap and let it rest in the fridge for 30 minutes Roll out the pastry on a floured surface to an 18 × 6 inch (45 × 15 cm) rectangle shape that is about ¼ inch (5 mm) thick.

MAKE THE SAUSAGE ROLLS

First combine the egg, milk, and turmeric to make the turmeric egg wash.

Shape the pork mixture into a sausage and lay it along the long side of the pastry, about 1 inch (3 cm) in from the edge. Brush the edge of the pastry with the egg wash and fold the pastry over the top of the filling to enclose it. Crimp the edges using a fork and slash the top of the pastry diagonally.

Lightly brush the pastry with the turmeric egg wash, then scatter over the kalonji seeds.

Place the sausage roll in the fridge for 10 minutes or so to firm up.

Preheat the oven to 400°F (200°C, or gas mark 6).

With a serrated knife, cut the sausage roll into desired lengths and place on a baking tray lined with parchment paper. Bake in the oven for 35 to 45 minutes, until they are golden brown.

Remove from the oven and place on a wire rack to cool. Store in an airtight container for 3 to 4 days.

Turkey Kebabs

A meat the whole family can agree on, turkey also works really well with Indian flavors. These are a little more fun than the usual kebab, with the addition of pepper for color and texture.

Makes 8

1 medium onion, minced

1 pound (500 g) ground turkey

¼ green pepper, finely diced

¼ red pepper, finely diced

handful of fresh coriander, finely chopped

1 teaspoon cumin seeds, ground

1 teaspoon pink salt (or chaat masala)

1 teaspoon chilli powder

1 teaspoon garam masala

1 tablespoon corn flour

Blitz the onion in a blender until fine (not a paste), or dice very finely.

Mix together the turkey, onion, peppers, coriander, all the spices, and corn flour. Combine it with your hands; if it feels too wet, add a little more corn flour.

Refrigerate for an hour or so. Meanwhile, soak wooden skewers in water.

With your hands, form the turkey mixture into flat oval shapes about ½ to ¾ inch (1 to 2 cm) thick. Hold the meat flat on your hand and thread the skewer into the meat and place on a plate. (Refrigerate the mixture again if it becomes too loose and hard to work with.) This should make eight to ten skewers.

Refrigerate the kebabs until you are ready to cook them.

Heat a large frying pan with a little oil on medium heat and gently pick up the meat (not the skewer as the meat may fall off) of a kebab. Place it in the pan and cook for 3 to 4 on minutes each side until golden.

Pudina Lamb Cutlets

I've cooked these for a number of events, and they are always a hit. The marinade is spectacular considering it's such a simple mixture of ingredients. The Kashmiri chilli powder adds a wonderful red tinge that comes to life with the pudina (or mint).

Serves 4

1 rack of lamb (8 cutlets)

1 inch (3 cm) piece of fresh ginger

3 garlic cloves

2 tablespoons (30 ml) malt vinegar

1 teaspoon Kashmiri chilli powder (or use half chilli powder and half paprika)

1 teaspoon salt

2 tablespoons (30 ml) vegetable oil

1 teaspoon black pepper, crushed

dried mint

Cut the rack into individual cutlets. Flatten them out a little using the back of your knife or a rolling pin.

Mince the ginger and garlic in a blender to make a paste.

In a bowl, combine the vinegar, ginger and garlic paste, chilli powder, salt, oil, and pepper.

Add the cutlets to the bowl. Marinate for about 30 minutes.

Heat your griddle until it's smoking and place the marinated cutlets on to cook. After about 4 minutes, turn them and cook for another 2 minutes.

Remove them from the griddle and let them rest for a few minutes.

Serve with a dusting of dried mint and a blob of Avocado and Spinach Yogurt (page 149).

Twisted Buffalo Wings

I am a wing fanatic—I love them with a dry rub, with chilli sauces, sticky, Asian style, hot and spicy, curried, roasted, you name it. This wing recipe is one I have tried to perfect for many years. I've laid it out here in two stages so you can have the wings with just the dry rub or you can make the sticky sauce too. Two for one!

Makes 12

10 to 15 chicken wings, skin on

3 tablespoons (23 g) plain flour

1 teaspoon paprika

2½ teaspoons garlic salt

1 teaspoon chilli powder, or to taste

1 teaspoon black pepper

½ teaspoon salt

1 tablespoon (14 g) butter

CHILLI SAUCE

3 to 4 Kashmiri chillies, soaked in hot water

1-inch (3 cm) piece of fresh ginger, roughly chopped

2 tablespoons (30 ml) rapeseed oil

1 teaspoon cumin seeds

4 garlic cloves, minced

1 tablespoon (15 ml) soy sauce

sea salt to taste (if required)

2 spring or green onions, finely sliced for garnish

large pinch of coriander, chopped

Prep the wings by removing the tip and cutting at the joint. Leave the skin on.

Mix the flour with all the spices in a bowl and coat the wings really well.

Shake and set to one side.

Preheat the oven to 400°F (200°C, or gas mark 6).

Line a baking tray with foil and spread the butter on the foil.

Place the floured wings on top and cook for about 15 minutes. Turn them over and cook for another 10 minutes or until crisp and cooked through.

CHILLI SAUCE

In a blender, mince the soaked chillies with the fresh ginger to make a paste.

Heat the oil on medium heat and stir in the cumin seeds until fragrant.

Add the garlic and sauté until it just starts to color (be careful it doesn't burn).

Pour in the chilli and ginger paste and cook for a minute until the oil separates. Stir in the soy sauce and a tiny splash of water if required. Check the seasoning and adjust if required.

Pour over the cooked wings and bake at 400°F (200°C, or gas mark 6) for another 5 minutes.

Top with sliced spring onions and coriander and serve.

Makes 4

FENUGREEK GARLIC BUTTER

6 tablespoons (90 g) salted butter, softened

2 teaspoons dried fenugreek leaves (kasoori methi), finely chopped

2 garlic cloves, very finely minced or grated

CHICKEN BOMB

1 tablespoon fresh ginger, grated

3 garlic cloves, minced

2 green chillies, finely chopped

14 ounces (400 g) ground chicken

1 teaspoon Kashmiri chilli powder

2 ounces (50 g) cheddar cheese, grated

1 teaspoon cumin seeds

1 teaspoon salt

handful of fresh mint

handful of coriander stems

1 tablespoon (15 ml) oil

2 teaspoons garam masala

1 egg

5 tablespoons (39 g) flour

2 cups (220 g) bread crumbs

FENUGREEK GARLIC BUTTER

Place ingredients in a bowl and mix until combined.

Scrape the mixed butter onto a sheet of plastic wrap or parchment paper and roughly shape into a cylinder and place in the freezer until firm.

CHICKEN BOMB

Blend the ginger, garlic, and chillies.

Put the ground chicken into a bowl and add the ginger, garlic, and chillies. Sprinkle in the chilli powder, cheese, cumin seeds, and salt.

Very finely chop the mint and coriander stems and mix into the chicken mixture.

Add the oil and garam masala, and mix it all together. Let the mixture rest in the fridge for at least 30 minutes.

Cut the garlic and fenugreek butter into 2-inch (5 cm) discs.

Crack an egg into a bowl and whisk, and put the flour and bread crumbs in two separate wide bowls.

Wet your hands (to prevent the meat from sticking to your fingers), scoop a handful of the ground chicken mixture, and flatten it in your hands. Place the butter disc into the center and roll the mixture into a ball. Repeat with the remaining chicken, wetting your hands between each one. Place the balls in the fridge for 10 minutes to firm up.

Coat the chicken balls in the flour and shake off the excess.

Coat each ball in the whisked egg, dripping off the excess, and then in the bread crumbs, pressing to adhere.

Put the coated chicken balls in the fridge for 30 minutes until firm to handle.

Preheat the oven to 350°F (180°C, or gas mark 4) and place a rack on a tray.

In a wok or small pan, pour oil deep enough to cover the chicken balls. Heat to 375°F (190°C).

Carefully place each chicken bomb into the oil and cook one ball at a time until it turns golden and crispy.

Place the chicken bomb on a rack and bake for 10 minutes. Let the chicken rest for 2 minutes before serving on a bed of butter sauce.

Top Tip • Keep an extra fenugreek garlic butter stick in the freezer. Stuff the butter into a chicken breast before breading it—Chicken Kiev with a Hari twist. These chicken bombs can also be frozen for a quick weeknight dinner.

Tandoori Tray Bake

A tray bake, as we call it in the United Kingdom, is a great way to feed the family in one hit. (They've recently become popular in the United States under the name "sheet pan dinners.") Though beloved for their simplicity, they still need to be super tasty to please everyone. I quite often do tandoori chicken with salad, corn, and potato wedges, but this all-in-one tray bake covers all the bases. Oh, and the roasted lemon adds a zingy sweetness, so make sure you squeeze that over the chicken!

Serves 4

MARINADE

1 large lemon

4 garlic cloves, crushed

¾-inch (2 cm) piece of fresh ginger, grated

1 green chilli, finely chopped

¾ cup (200 g) Greek yogurt

1 teaspoon salt

1 teaspoon garam masala

1 teaspoon cumin seeds, crushed

1 tablespoon Kashmiri red chilli powder

1 tablespoon dried fenugreek leaves (kasoori methi)

8 pieces of chicken drumsticks and/or thighs, skinned

1 pound (500 g) new potatoes

2 corns on the cob, cut into 3 pieces

1 red onion, cut into wedges

1 lemon, cut into wedges

1 teaspoon cumin seeds

1 tablespoon (15 ml) mustard oil

salt to taste

1 green pepper, cut into chunks

1 red pepper, cut into chunks

GARNISH

fresh coriander

sliced red onion

red chilli, sliced (optional)

Mix all the marinade ingredients in a bowl so they are fully combined.

Slash the chicken pieces to the bone and place in the bowl with the marinade, fully coating the pieces. Marinate in the fridge as long as possible, overnight if you can.

Preheat the oven to 350°F (180°C, or gas mark 4).

Slice each of the new potatoes halfway down but not all the way through (hassleback) 3 or 4 times, to pick up the flavors while cooking. Place in a large roasting pan with the pieces of corn, onion, and lemon wedges.

Place the marinated chicken in between the vegetables and drizzle over the mustard oil, cumin seeds, and a sprinkling of salt.

Place in the hot oven and bake for 30 minutes. Then add the pepper chunks and cook for an additional 15 to 20 minutes until cooked and the chicken has crisped up.

To serve, sprinkle with coriander, sliced onion, and red chilli slices (optional).

Top Tip • You can also add mushrooms, paneer, butternut squash, or any other veg of your choice.

Spiced Battered Fish

As a kid we had fish and chips from the chip shop every Friday—it was the only day we got to enjoy a Western meal at home, and it was always a real treat. This dish is a take on classic British fish and chips, but the fish is marinated with north Indian spices. Many people think that white fish is too delicate to work with Indian spices, but tell that to the millions of Indians who enjoy fish every day!

Serves 4

1½-inch (4 cm) piece of
    fresh ginger

4 garlic cloves

2 lemons

½ teaspoon turmeric powder

1 teaspoon cumin seeds, crushed

1 teaspoon coriander seeds,
    crushed

1 teaspoon carom seeds
    (ajwain seeds)

1 teaspoon Kashmiri chilli powder

salt to taste

1½ cups (200 g) gram flour
    (chickpea flour)

water

14 ounces (400 g) firm white fish
    in thick portions

oil for deep-frying

Crush the ginger and garlic to a paste with a mortar and pestle and squeeze in the juice from 1 lemon. Add to a large bowl.

Cut the second lemon into wedges to serve with the fish.

Add the turmeric and crushed cumin and coriander seeds to the bowl with the carom seeds, chilli powder, and salt.

Sieve in the gram flour, and mix all the ingredients together, adding a little water to make a thick batter.

Place the fish in the batter and coat all the pieces—marinate for about 30 minutes.

Begin to heat the oil in a fryer to 350°F (180°C). Check if the oil is hot enough by dropping a little batter into the oil. If it bubbles and floats to the top straightaway, it's ready.

Very gently place the battered fish into the oil (place it away from you so the hot oil doesn't splash up).

Fry the fish until it's cooked through and each piece is golden and crispy (about 5 to 6 minutes).

Remove and place on paper towels to drain. Serve hot with homemade chips and a wedge of lemon.

Top Tip • To make this vegan, use banana blossom (available in cans)—it's the perfect alternative to fish. Coat it in the flour mixture before adding the water. Then simply add the water to make the batter, and coat with the batter and fry in the same way.

Aloo Tikki Topped with Tandoori King Prawns

Aloo tikki (or Indian spicy potato cakes) make a great snack on their own and are sold on street corners in India as a quick bite or served with spiced chickpeas as a mini salad. They can be played down as a burger patty or jazzed up as a posh little starter for a special occasion. Try them topped with a juicy marinated king prawn—they will definitely impress.

Serves 4

12 large uncooked king prawns

1-inch (3 cm) piece of fresh ginger

2 garlic cloves

1 fresh chilli, chopped

½ teaspoon chilli powder

1 teaspoon salt

juice of 1 lemon

⅓ cup (100 g) yogurt

1 teaspoon mustard oil plus
   1 tablespoon (15 ml) to cook
   the prawns

1 teaspoon garam masala

ALOO TIKKI

4 medium potatoes, washed
   with skin on

1 teaspoon salt

1 teaspoon garam masala

1 teaspoon cumin seeds

2 chillies, finely chopped

2 tablespoons (16 g) fresh ginger,
   grated

handful of fresh coriander leaves,
   chopped

GARNISH

half a lemon

handful of coriander, finely
   chopped

PRAWNS

Slice down the back of each prawn and use a toothpick to pull out the dark vein. Wash and dry on paper towels.

Crush the ginger, garlic, and chilli with a mortar and pestle to make a paste.

Place the prawns in a large bowl and sprinkle with the chilli powder, salt, lemon juice, and the crushed ginger and garlic. Set to one side.

Blend the yogurt, 1 teaspoon oil, and garam masala together and add to the prawns. Mix and ensure they are fully coated. Refrigerate until required.

ALOO TIKKI

Place the potatoes with the skin on in a pan, cover with cold water, and bring to a boil. Reduce the heat and gently cook until soft. Drain and allow to cool.

Once cooled, peel the skin off with your fingers and discard. Grate the potatoes into a bowl.

Add the salt, garam masala, cumin seeds, chillies, ginger, and coriander, and mix together.

Wet your hands so the potato mixture doesn't stick to your fingers, and begin to shape the potato mixture into small patties or tikki, roughly 1½ to 2 inches (4 to 5 cm) in diameter and about 1 inch (3 cm) thick.

Heat a little oil in a frying pan or tawa (Indian griddle pan) on medium heat.

Place the cakes in the pan and cook until golden brown. Turn them over and cook the other side.

Once the tikki are almost cooked, heat 1 tablespoon mustard oil in a frying pan on high heat and fry the prawns for 3 to 4 minutes until they turn pink.

Once the tikki are crisp on both sides, top each with a dollop of Indian Tomato Ketchup (page 143) and a prawn, and squeeze over lemon juice and fresh coriander to serve.

Barbecue Pulled Lamb Burger

If you love a low, slow cook, this is a wonderful way to use lamb shoulder. (You could also use pork butt or beef shin, if you prefer.) The dry rub is a great way to get those smoky flavors penetrating into the joint.

Serves 8-10

SPICE RUB

2 tablespoons (36 g) salt

1 tablespoon Kashmiri chilli powder

1 tablespoon cumin seeds, crushed

1 tablespoon coriander seeds, crushed

1 tablespoon (15 g) muscovado brown sugar

4½ pounds (2 kg) lamb shoulder

SPICY BARBECUE SAUCE

1 onion, sliced

5 garlic cloves

1½-inch (4 cm) piece of fresh ginger, grated

handful of dried apricots, roughly chopped

7 tablespoons (100 ml) vinegar

⅔ cup (150 ml) orange juice

2 to 4 red chillies, chopped

4 tomatoes, roughly chopped

TO SERVE

handful of pomegranate seeds

fresh coriander, chopped

2 red chillies, sliced (optional)

8–10 brioche rolls, toasted

Mix the dry rub ingredients in a bowl.

Score the meat and rub the spice mix all over. Set to one side.

Preheat the oven to 275°F (135°C, or gas mark 1).

Slice the onion and place into an oven tray. Add the garlic, ginger, apricots, vinegar, orange juice, chillies, and tomatoes. Place the lamb on top and cover the tray tightly with foil.

Place it in the oven, and cook for 4 hours.

After 4 hours, remove the foil, take the lamb out, and pour the juices from the tray into a pan.

Place the lamb back in the oven and cook for another 30 minutes.

Heat the juices in the pan, and simmer until thickened.

Pour some of the sauce over the lamb and cook for 10 to 15 minutes more. Remove from the oven and let the meat rest.

You should be able to pull the bone straight out of the lamb shoulder. Shred the lamb using two forks and stir in more of the thickened sauce. Keep some to serve on the side.

Sprinkle over a handful of pomegranate seeds, chopped coriander, and sliced chillies and load onto toasted rolls. Serve with my Indian Slaw (page 151).

Top Tip • Try this recipe with different cuts of meat.

Bunny Chow

This is South Africa's answer to the curry and a tiffin (a light teatime meal) all in one, and a great example of how food and flavors travel across the globe. It was created by Indian migrant workers in Durban; in fact, "bunny chow" is South African slang for "Gujarati food." It's thought that Indian laborers working the sugar cane plantations carried their curry lunches to the field in hollowed loaves of bread, which made for a delicious and wholesome all-in-one meal.

A classic bunny chow is pretty hot, with a distinctly African curry flavor that departs a bit from an Indian curry. This is because the Indian migrants couldn't obtain all the ingredients they needed to re-create the flavors of home, so they adapted with locally sourced ingredients. In this recipe, I used individual spices, but feel free to use a hot curry powder instead!

Serves 4-6

1 tablespoon (15 ml) rapeseed oil

3-inch (7 cm) piece of cassia bark

6 green cardamom pods

4 cloves

1 bay leaf

1 teaspoon fennel seeds

10 curry leaves

1 large onion, finely diced

6 garlic cloves, minced

1 tablespoon (15 ml) white vinegar

2 teaspoons sugar

1 tablespoon fresh ginger, grated

2 to 4 green chillies, diced

½ teaspoon turmeric

1 teaspoon garam masala

1 teaspoon Kashmiri chilli powder

1 teaspoon cumin seeds, ground

1 teaspoon coriander seeds, ground

2 pounds (1 kg) lamb neck fillet or leg, diced, or 6 chicken thighs (skinned, boned, and chopped)

1 teaspoon salt or to taste

5 small to medium potatoes, quartered

2 tomatoes, puréed

handful of fresh coriander leaves, chopped

TO SERVE

4 medium crusty buns

TOPPINGS (OPTIONAL)

chopped tomatoes or tomato kachumber

sliced red onion rings or Punjabi piyaz

sliced green chillies

Greek yogurt or cucumber raita

Heat the oil on medium heat in a pot and add the cassia bark, cardamom, cloves, bay leaf, and fennel seeds, and stir until fragrant.

Add the curry leaves and diced onion. Turn the heat high for a few minutes, stir, and then reduce to a medium heat and cook for 15 to 20 minutes until golden brown.

Add the minced garlic and cook for 3 to 4 minutes.

Stir in the vinegar and sugar, and then add the grated ginger and diced chillies.

Add the turmeric, garam masala, chilli powder, ground cumin, and ground coriander.

Stir in the meat and salt, and coat the meat with the spices.

Cover and cook on low heat for 20 minutes, stirring occasionally.

Add the potatoes and cook for another 20 minutes before adding the pureed tomatoes.

Leave for another 20 minutes until the meat is tender and the potatoes are soft. Remove from the heat and stir in the chopped coriander.

TO SERVE

Hollow out the inner part of each bun, keeping it intact.

Scoop the curry into the bunny and serve with tomato kachumber, red onion rings, sliced green chillies, and yogurt or raita on the side.

Banana Blossom Cutlet

This is exactly what it sounds like: the banana flower, also known as the banana heart. The next vegan diner's dream, it's a purple-skinned flower that grows on the end of a cluster of the banana fruit and looks a bit like an artichoke. The pretty tear-shaped ingredient has been part of Indian and Southeast Asian cuisine for many years. While it can be eaten raw, what makes the blossom spectacular is that when cooked the chunky flesh flakes just like fish; and although it has a neutral taste, its fibrous nature means that it can take on strong flavors and seasoning. You can find it canned, fresh, or frozen.

Serves 4

1 medium potato

14 ounces (400 g) canned banana blossom, chopped

1 tablespoon coconut oil

1 small onion, diced

4 garlic cloves, chopped

20 curry leaves

1½-inch (4 cm) piece of fresh ginger, grated

1 green chilli, chopped

½ teaspoon turmeric powder

1 teaspoon black pepper, ground

1 teaspoon garam masala

1 teaspoon salt (or to taste)

2 tablespoons (15 g) plain flour

½ cup (60 g) bread crumbs

oil to fry

Boil the potato until it's soft, and then grate it. Set aside for later.

Drain the blossom and roughly chop.

Heat coconut oil in a pan, add the diced onion, and sauté for 5 minutes before adding the garlic.

Stir in the curry leaves and cook until golden. Add the ginger and green chilli, and cook for a few minutes.

Sprinkle in the turmeric and add the chopped banana blossom. Stir and sauté until the mixture dries out.

Add the black pepper with the garam masala and salt. Remove from the heat and allow to cool. Add the grated potato and mix thoroughly.

Once it's cool enough to handle, wet your hands and shape into patties.

Make a thin batter with water and plain flour.

Dip the cutlets in this flour batter to lightly coat, and then coat in the bread crumbs.

Pour enough oil to shallowly cover the bottom of a pan and place over medium to high heat.

Fry the patties on both sides until golden brown. Drain on paper towels. Serve with a mango salsa.

Keema Pie with Fluffy Spiced Mash & Spring Onions

There is simply nothing more homey and satisfying than shepherd's pie—and as a bonus, it's a great one-tray meal for the whole family. Filled with succulent meat in a delicious gravy and loads of vegetables and topped with creamy mashed potatoes—for me, it ticks all the boxes except for spice, so I always have mine with a huge dollop of chilli sauce on the side. I thought about how I could add my own little twist, and this recipe is what I came up with. I like to use ground lamb, but pork, chicken, or beef will work just as well.

Serves 4

2 tablespoons (30 ml) oil

1 onion, finely diced

3 garlic cloves, finely chopped

14 ounces (400 g) canned plum tomatoes

1 tablespoon fresh ginger, grated

1 teaspoon cumin seeds, crushed

1 teaspoon salt

½ teaspoon turmeric

1 to 2 chillies, finely chopped (optional)

10 mushrooms, quartered

1¼ pounds (600 g) lean ground lamb

3½ ounces (100 g) frozen peas

MASALA MASH

7 large Maris Piper or russet potatoes, peeled and chopped into chunks

½ teaspoon salt

2½ tablespoons (40 g) butter

3 tablespoons (45 ml) milk

1 teaspoon garam masala

GARNISH

handful of fresh coriander leaves, chopped

2 spring or green onions, chopped

Heat the oil on medium heat in a wide-based pan and add the diced onion. Sauté for 5 minutes before adding the garlic. Stir and continue to cook for about 10 minutes until the onions are golden brown in color. If the onion catches, reduce the heat and add a dash of water.

Reduce the heat and add the tomatoes, ginger, cumin, salt, turmeric, and chillies (optional).

Stir together and cook to reduce until the tomatoes break down into the sauce (about 5 minutes). All the ingredients should melt together with the spices, creating the aromatic masala paste.

Turn the heat up, add the mushrooms, and cook for a few minutes before adding the lamb.

Stir to coat the lamb with the sauce. Once coated, reduce the heat and cook for about 15 minutes.

Stir in the frozen peas and cook for an additional 5 minutes.

Remove from the heat and spoon into a casserole dish. Allow to cool.

MASALA MASH

Preheat your oven to 350°F (180°C, or gas mark 4). Cover the potatoes with cold water and add a little salt. Bring this to a boil, and then reduce the heat. Cook the potatoes until soft. Once cooked, drain and place back in the pan.

Add a little salt and butter and pour in a little milk (add more if required) and mash the potatoes to create a firm mash.

Sprinkle in the garam masala.

Place the masala mash on top of the lamb mixture and place in the oven. Bake for about 25 to 30 minutes until it's bubbling.

To serve, sprinkle with fresh coriander and chopped spring onions.

Steak 'n' Spice

If you love your steak with a dash of Tabasco, then you are going to *love* this. It's a superb way to introduce an Indian twist to steak, a lamb chop, or a pork joint. Happily, this is also one of those recipes that makes life easy. Gentle spicing tenderizes the meat and beautifully flavors it at the same time, a bit like the galavat technique (page 14) discussed in the Introduction. All you need to serve this is a luxurious side salad and thick-cut chips.

Serves 2

1 tablespoon fresh ginger, grated

1 small onion, roughly chopped

3 garlic cloves

2 teaspoons coriander seeds

1 teaspoon cumin seeds

1 teaspoon black mustard seeds

1 teaspoon Kashmiri chilli powder

1 teaspoon salt

3 tablespoons (45 ml) vegetable oil

2 rib eye steaks

1 tablespoon (14 g) butter

Place the ginger, onion, and garlic in a food processor and blend until it's finely minced.

Grind the coriander, cumin, and mustard seeds in a spice grinder. Stir in the chilli powder and salt.

Heat 1 tablespoon (15 ml) of oil over medium heat and add the onion mixture. Sauté gently for 2 to 3 minutes. Remove from the heat and add the ground spices. Mix through until fragrant.

Once cooled, smear the onion and spice mixture over the steaks. Cover in plastic wrap and refrigerate for up to 24 hours.

To cook the steaks, heat a pan or griddle on high heat and place the steaks in the pan. Reduce the heat to medium so the spices don't burn and sear for 2 to 3 minutes, turn them over, and add some butter. Cook to the desired level.

When the steaks are cooked, remove from the heat and let them stand for 5 to 6 minutes.

Thinly slice the steak against the grain to serve.

Top Tip • Try this with my version of chimichurri (page 147).

Pepperoni Naanza

A slight Indian twist on a classic Italian pizza. A basic naan dough that includes a sprinkling of turmeric goodness with peppery kalongi seeds makes the base vibrant yellow and crisp. It's dressed with a full-flavored tomato masala and then topped with all the usual favorites: pepperoni, sliced red onion, olives, diced paneer, and mozzarella. What could be better?

Makes 4

1 teaspoon dried active yeast

1 teaspoon sugar

1¾ cups (200 g) plain flour

1 teaspoon black onion seeds

½ teaspoon salt

½ teaspoon baking powder

½ teaspoon turmeric

1 tablespoon (15 ml) vegetable oil

2 tablespoons (30 g) plain yogurt

2 tablespoons (30 ml) milk

MASALA

2 tablespoons (30 ml) oil

2 onions, finely diced

1 teaspoon salt

1 heaped tablespoon fresh ginger, grated

1 chilli, finely chopped (optional)

3 garlic cloves, finely chopped

14 ounces (400 g) canned plum tomatoes, puréed

1 teaspoon turmeric

1 teaspoon chilli powder

1 teaspoon garam masala

handful of fresh coriander leaves, chopped

TOPPINGS (OPTIONAL)

shredded mozzarella

diced paneer

shredded cheddar cheese

pepperoni slices

red onion, sliced

black olives

red chilli, sliced

coriander, chopped

In a small bowl, mix the yeast and sugar with a tablespoon of warm water to activate. Leave for 5 minutes in a warm place until frothy.

Meanwhile, in a separate bowl, mix the flour, onion seeds, salt, baking powder, and turmeric. When the yeast is frothy, add it to the flour with the oil and yogurt.

Knead the dough with slightly wet hands, folding as you go, or use a stand mixer if you prefer. If it feels a little dry, add some milk and continue to knead. Once it's nice and soft, cover with plastic wrap and leave it in a warm place to rise for at least 1 hour.

MASALA

Heat the oil in a pan on high heat and add the diced onions. Sauté and stir—if it starts to stick, just add a little water and stir. Add the salt to help the onions cook.

Put the ginger, chilli, and garlic into a blender and blend to a paste (add a little water if required).

After 10 minutes of cooking, the onions should have started to brown. Now stir in the ginger, chilli, and garlic paste.

Once softened, add the puréed canned tomatoes and increase the heat until the tomatoes start to simmer.

Reduce the heat and add the turmeric, chilli powder, and garam masala. Cook until the masala is thick.

MAKE THE NAANZA

Preheat the oven to 400°F (200°C, or gas mark 6) and insert an oven tray or pizza stone to heat up.

Divide the dough into four balls, and place on a floured surface. Roll each into a tear shape, about ¼ inch (0.5 cm) thick.

Transfer to the hot baking tray and work quickly, smearing on the masala sauce, sprinkling over the cheese, and then adding the toppings of your choice. Top off with a little more cheese.

Place in the oven to cook until the dough turns golden and the cheese bubbles (approximately 2 to 5 minutes). Sprinkle over a little coriander and serve.

Curried Butternut Squash Soup

Rich, creamy, and full of flavor—soup fans will love this because it is packed with the natural sweet goodness of winter squash, and with a little chilli, it warms you from the inside out. It's the perfect fall family pleaser, but it also makes a great little starter for a party. This recipe works beautifully with pumpkin too.

Serves 2 as a main dish or 4 as a starter

1 butternut squash
1 teaspoon cumin seeds
1 red onion, chopped
2 garlic cloves, minced
1-inch (3 cm) piece of fresh ginger, grated
2 red chillies, chopped (keep some for garnish)
2 cups (500 ml) chicken stock or water
4 tablespoons (50 g) coconut cream

Preheat the oven to 350°F (180°C, or gas mark 4).

Slice the squash into four long strips, remove the seeds, and place on a tray with a little knob of butter on each. Roast in the oven for about 35 minutes until soft.

Meanwhile, heat the oil in a pan over medium heat and add the cumin seeds, stirring until fragrant. Then add the onions and gently cook until soft.

Stir in the garlic, ginger, and chillies and cook for about 5 minutes.

Once the squash is soft, scrape the flesh out and discard the skin. Stir the flesh into the onions.

Add the stock and cook through until everything is soft (about 5 minutes).

Using a hand blender or immersion blender, blitz the soup until it's smooth and thick. Pour in the coconut cream. If it's too thick, add a little hot water.

Pour into bowls and top with a swirl of coconut cream and a chopped chilli. Serve with some crisp naan bread.

Top Tip • You can use the seeds from the squash or pumpkin as a spiced topper for your soup: Remove the seeds from one pumpkin; wash and dry them on paper towels. Spread the seeds on an oven tray and pour 2 teaspoons of oil over them. Rub to coat them with the oil and sprinkle with 1 teaspoon each of salt and chilli flakes. Roast in the oven for 10 minutes at 350°F (180°C, or gas mark 4) until they are golden brown. After they have cooled, store in an airtight jar and use as needed.

Dhal & Aubergine Moussaka

A classic Greek moussaka is made with spiced lamb and sliced eggplant, but by substituting black lentils for the meat, you can make a wonderfully versatile vegetarian option. The lentils not only add texture, but they soak up the aromatics of the ginger, garlic, and nutmeg. I have added a few extra spices that also combine well with the earthy nature of the lentils.

Serves 4-6

LENTIL MASALA

1 to 2 tablespoons (15 to 30 ml) vegetable oil

1 stick of cassia bark

1 teaspoon cumin seeds

1 medium onion, finely chopped

3 garlic cloves, sliced

3 fresh tomatoes, chopped

1-inch (3 cm) piece of fresh ginger, grated

2 green chillies, chopped

½ teaspoon turmeric powder

1 teaspoon chilli powder

2 teaspoons coriander seeds, crushed

3½ ounces (100 g) soaked uncooked urad dhal (whole black lentils) or 14 ounces (400 g) precooked lentils

salt to taste

1 to 2 tablespoons (14 to 28 g) butter

1 teaspoon garam masala

½ teaspoon nutmeg

1 teaspoon dried fenugreek leaf (kasoori methi)

handful of fresh coriander leaves, chopped

Heat the oil in a pressure cooker (if using uncooked lentils), and add the cassia bark and cumin seeds. When the cumin seeds sizzle, add the chopped onions and garlic. On medium heat, fry until golden brown.

Stir in the chopped tomatoes, ginger, green chillies, turmeric, chilli powder, and crushed coriander seeds.

Stir in 3½ ounces (100 g) of the soaked urad dhal (whole black lentils) and pour in 2 cups (500 ml) of water with a teaspoon of salt (or to taste).

Put the lid on and bring the temperature to high. Reduce the heat and simmer for 25 minutes. (If using cooked lentils, simmer until heated through.)

Turn the heat off and allow the pressure to subside. Remove the lid and stir. Test that the lentils are cooked through (they should be soft and squeeze between your fingers).

If the lentils are still watery, simmer and stir on a gentle heat until they thicken and start to get creamy.

Remove from the heat and take out the cassia bark. Stir in the butter, garam masala, nutmeg, and fenugreek leaf.

Stir in the fresh coriander leaves and set to one side.

Preheat the oven to 350°F (180°C, or gas mark 4).

CUMIN-GRIDDLED EGGPLANT

As the lentils are cooking, heat a griddle on high heat.

Mix the crushed cumin seeds with the oil. Drizzle over the eggplant slices and cook on the griddle until they begin to color and soften.

TURMERIC BECHAMEL

In a large saucepan, heat butter over medium-high heat until melted.

Stir in flour, turmeric, salt, and pepper. Cook until golden.

Gradually pour in the warmed milk, whisking continuously. Continue cooking, stirring occasionally, over medium heat for 5 to 7 minutes.

Whisk the eggs and pour into the bechamel mixture while stirring. Add the nutmeg.

continued next page ▶

5

Cheeky Curries

There's nothing more satisfying than a curry! Each dish is a unique experience. I've included several different flavor profiles here, hoping to show you how you can put spices and ingredients together in different formats to reveal the many layers of curry complexity.

Lamb Balti

Bold and brash is the only way to describe a balti, which is said to have originated in the United Kingdom by Indian migrants who worked in curry houses in the 1970s. The balti is actually the name of the dish it's cooked and served in; it's made of aluminum and has two handles similar to that of a cast-iron karahi. Serve with a fluffy naan to mop up the delicious sauce.

Serves 4-6

1½ teaspoons cumin seeds

1 tablespoon coriander seeds

1-inch (3 cm) piece of fresh ginger

6 garlic cloves

2 tomatoes, quartered

1½ teaspoons garam masala

1½ teaspoons turmeric

1 teaspoon Kashmiri chilli powder

1 tablespoon (15 g) full-fat Greek yogurt

salt, to taste

2 tablespoons (30 ml) rapeseed oil

1 teaspoon brown mustard seeds

1 bay leaf

1 onion, finely chopped

6 to 10 whole green chillies (reduce if this is too many for you)

1¼ pounds (600 g) lamb neck fillet, cut into 1-inch (3 cm) pieces

1 teaspoon black peppercorns, freshly ground

1 tablespoon (15 ml) lemon juice, or to taste

large handful of fresh coriander leaves, finely chopped

Grind the cumin and coriander seeds, and set aside. Crush the ginger and garlic with a mortar and pestle.

Blend the tomatoes to a purée and stir in the ground spices, garam masala, turmeric, chilli powder, yogurt, and salt.

Heat the oil in a nonstick saucepan (or karahi) and add the mustard seeds. Once they pop, add the bay leaf and chopped onion. Stir and cook on medium heat.

After about 15 minutes, add the crushed ginger and garlic with the green chillies, and cook for at least 20 minutes until the onions are well browned. If the onions catch, add a splash of water and continue to cook.

Stir in the tomato mixture. Turn the heat up and stir until the sauce thickens and you are left with a thick masala paste (10 to 15 minutes).

Add the lamb pieces, coating with the masala. Reduce the heat and place the lid on the pan. Cook for about 40 minutes, stirring occasionally.

The meat will produce a thick gravy. Add a little hot water to loosen it, or stir-fry on high heat to thicken further, depending on how you like it.

Once the meat is tender, add black pepper and a squeeze of lemon.

Check the seasoning and stir in the chopped coriander. Serve with fresh naan (page 134).

Bhuna Gosht

This dish is named after the traditional cooking method used to make it. It uses a cacophony of whole spices that are toasted to heighten their aromatics and blended to create a delicious mix. The "bhun" comes at the end of the cooking process, where the masala is reduced on high heat and continually stirred to intensify the flavors. This requires a little elbow grease, so be prepared to work for your supper.

Serves 4-6

2 pounds (900 g) leg of lamb or mutton, trimmed and chopped

SPICE BLEND

2 teaspoons cumin seeds

3 teaspoons coriander seeds

2 teaspoons mustard seeds

2 teaspoons fennel seeds

1 teaspoon fenugreek seeds

2 to 3 dried red chillies

MASALA

1 tablespoon (15 ml) rapeseed oil

2 onions, finely chopped

6 garlic cloves, finely chopped

20 curry leaves

1½-inch (4 cm) piece of fresh ginger, grated

2 to 3 green chillies, sliced in half (optional)

14 ounces (400 g) canned plum tomatoes

1 teaspoon salt

½ teaspoon turmeric

1 teaspoon garam masala

handful of fresh coriander leaves, chopped

Heat a frying pan over medium heat and add the cumin, coriander, mustard, fennel, and fenugreek seeds, and the dried chillies. Keep the spices moving for a minute or two until they become aromatic. Empty the spices into a bowl and let them cool before grinding to a fine powder in a coffee grinder or with a mortar and pestle. Set aside.

Heat the oil and onions in a large pan over high heat, adding the garlic after a few minutes. Sauté and if they stick, add a little water and continue to stir when required.

Once they have browned, add the curry leaves, ginger, green chillies (if using), tomatoes, and salt. Cook until the tomatoes break down, creating a thick paste.

Add the roasted spice mix and turmeric to the pan and stir well. Cook for a minute or two, taking care not to let the sauce catch on the bottom of the pan. If it feels dry, add a splash of water and quickly stir.

Place the meat in the pan and stir to coat on high heat, stir-frying for 5 minutes.

Reduce the heat, put a lid on the pan, and simmer for about 30 to 40 minutes (longer if using mutton). Check that the meat is tender. If it isn't, let it cook a while longer.

When the meat is ready, remove the lid from the pan, turn up the heat, and fry to reduce the sauce until it almost disappears. The aim is to intensify the flavor, creating a dry, concentrated sauce that clings tightly to the tender morsels of meat.

Finish with a sprinkle of garam masala and a handful of chopped fresh coriander.

Top Tip • This dish is great with more heat, so feel free to add more fresh chillies to make it hotter, if you wish.

Thari Wala Chicken

This is my go-to everyday curry. The first thing I learned to cook, it's rustic, homey, and the perfect dish for the whole family to enjoy. It's a versatile base masala that can be used in so many different ways. For me, it represents everything that is great about Indian food. The key is to allow your onions to brown until they are dark and moody brown in color!

Serves 4-6

8 to 10 pieces of chicken (4 to 5 legs cut into thighs and drumsticks)

TOMATO MASALA

2 tablespoons (30 ml) oil

2 onions, finely diced

3 garlic cloves, finely chopped

14 ounces (400 g) canned plum tomatoes

1 heaped tablespoon fresh ginger, grated

1 teaspoon salt

1 teaspoon turmeric

handful of fresh coriander stalks, finely chopped

1 chilli, finely chopped

1 teaspoon of garam masala

handful of fresh coriander leaves, chopped

Skin the chicken, removing any excess fat. Set aside.

Heat the oil in a pan and add the onions and garlic. Fry on high heat for a few minutes, and then reduce the heat and cook gently for about 20 to 30 minutes until they turn a lovely dark golden brown.

Once the onions are browned, add the canned tomatoes, ginger, salt, turmeric, coriander stalks, and chopped chilli. Increase the heat to high until it comes to a simmer, and then reduce to medium.

Let the onions and tomatoes melt together so they create a thick aromatic masala paste. This will take 5 to 10 minutes, so be patient!

Once the paste is shiny and thick and all the moisture has evaporated, add the chicken pieces and stir to coat.

Fry the chicken on high for 5 minutes.

Reduce the heat to the lowest setting and put the lid on the pan. Cook for 20 to 25 minutes until the chicken is cooked through and the meat is starting to fall away from the bone.

The meat will have created its own thick sauce. Either leave as is or if you like more sauce (like me), add enough boiling water to just cover the chicken and simmer for a few more minutes. Remove from the heat.

Stir in the garam masala and coriander leaves, and serve.

Top Tips

. Make the tomato masala in bulk and freeze in tubs for use during the week.

. Use chopped thigh fillets for a boneless version.

. Any meat of your choice will work with this masala.

. Add coconut milk for a creamy finish.

. Add tamarind for a tangy finish.

If the onions stick to the bottom of the pan, reduce the heat and add a dash of water. You can do this as many times as you need to. It also helps the onions to start breaking down.

Lamb Dhansak

This is a rustic one-pot lamb, lentil, and vegetable stew that's taken to new heights with the use of tangy tamarind and warming spices. Light, sweet, and savory, it's typically eaten with the whole family as a weekend meal.

Serves 4-6

LENTIL AND VEGETABLE MIXTURE

2 ounces (60 g) toor dhal (split pigeon peas)

2 ounces (60 g) masoor dhal (split red lentils)

2 ounces (60 g) urad dhal (split and dehusked black lentils)

1 small eggplant, chopped into large chunks

½ small pumpkin, chopped into large chunks (you could also use butternut squash or sweet potato)

1 medium onion, chopped in chunks

15 fresh mint leaves, chopped

DRY SPICES

1 teaspoon cumin seeds

1 teaspoon coriander seeds

1½-inch (4 cm) stick of cassia bark

4 green cardamom pods

4 whole black peppercorns

1 tablespoon dry fenugreek leaves

WET PASTE

6 garlic cloves

1-inch (3 cm) piece of fresh ginger

2 chillies

MASALA

2 tablespoons (30 ml) oil

2 medium onions, diced

1 teaspoon turmeric powder

3 tomatoes, diced

1 tablespoon (15 g) tamarind paste

1 teaspoon salt

1 pound (500 g) leg of lamb, trimmed and cut into chunks

handful of fresh coriander leaves, chopped

LENTIL AND VEGETABLE MIXTURE

Put all the lentils, vegetables, onions, and mint into a pan with 4¼ cups (1 L) of water and some salt. Bring this to a boil, and then simmer for 20 minutes until the lentils have cooked through.

DRY SPICES AND WET PASTE

Place all the dry spices into a spice grinder and blend to a fine powder.

Place this powder into a blender with the garlic, ginger, and chillies and grind to make an aromatic paste. Add a splash of water to loosen if required.

MASALA

Heat the oil over medium heat and fry the diced onions until they are golden brown (about 20 minutes).

Once the onions are browned, add the spice paste along with the turmeric and fry for a few minutes until golden.

Add the tomatoes, tamarind paste, and salt. Stir for about 5 minutes until the masala is thick and glossy.

On high heat, stir in the lamb and coat with the masala. After about 5 minutes, add the cooked lentil mixture and simmer on low heat for about 30 to 40 minutes. Make sure you occasionally stir as this can stick to the bottom of the pan.

Once the meat is tender, check the seasoning and adjust if required.

Sprinkle with the fresh coriander to serve.

Butter Chicken

Also called Murgh Makhani, this beloved dish is perfect for a weeknight family dinner. The sauce is rich, with a wonderfully creamy, smooth texture as well as an iconic vibrant orange color. There are so many different ways to cook this dish. You can change the recipe to make it healthier if you choose, but assuming you're not eating it every night, I believe it's better to indulge a little! You can also marinate the chicken first—just use the marinade from my Schmokin' Tandoori Wings recipe on page 32.

Serves 4-6

TOMATO SAUCE

2 medium red onions, roughly chopped

2 to 3 green chillies

1 teaspoon fresh ginger, grated

4 garlic cloves, roughly chopped

1½-inch (4 cm) stick of cassia bark

4 green cardamom pods

3 cloves

5 whole black peppercorns

1 teaspoon salt

7 ripe red tomatoes, roughly chopped, or 14 ounces (400 g) canned plum tomatoes

MASALA

2 tablespoons (30 ml) ghee or butter

1 tablespoon cumin seeds

½ teaspoon turmeric

1 teaspoon Kashmiri chilli powder

2 teaspoons coriander seeds, crushed (coriander powder)

8 chicken thighs or 4 breasts, skinned, trimmed, and cut into cubes

1 cup (240 ml) hot water

1 tablespoon honey

½ cup (100 ml) double cream, heavy cream, or yogurt

1 heaped tablespoon dried fenugreek leaves (kasoori methi)

1 tablespoon (15 g) butter

TOMATO SAUCE

Put the onions, chillies, ginger, garlic, cassia bark, green cardamom, cloves, peppercorns, and salt into a pan and cover with approximately 2 cups (500 ml) of water. Bring to a boil.

Add the tomatoes and simmer for 15 to 20 minutes on medium heat, stirring occasionally.

After the sauce has reduced and the mixture has thickened, remove the pan from the heat. Remove the cassia bark and let the mixture cool.

Blend to a fine sauce using a hand blender or immersion blender until it's smooth, thick, and creamy.

MASALA

In a second pan, heat the ghee or butter. Once melted, add the cumin seeds and as soon as you can smell the musky cumin aroma, reduce the heat and stir in the tomato sauce. Be very careful as this will spit and bubble so keep stirring. Cook for about 5 to 10 minutes until the butter and sauce come together.

Stir in turmeric, chilli powder, and crushed coriander seeds, and cook for 2 to 3 minutes. Reduce the heat and add the chicken to the pan, stir to coat, and simmer for 15 minutes on a gentle heat.

Add a little hot water to loosen, if required, and then add the honey. Cook for 5 minutes until the chicken is cooked through—the gravy should be a lovely bright orange color.

Remove from the heat and stir in the cream (or yogurt) and fenugreek.

Add a bit of butter or cream on top before serving.

Top Tip • Make it vegetarian with paneer and peppers! Do not substitute Kasoori methi for the spice—it will be too overpowering; instead add a teaspoon of garam masala.

Chettinad Chicken

A lovely, flavorful chicken curry dish from Tamil Nadu in South India, Chettinad Chicken is made by toasting spices with coconut and producing an aromatic masala that has a slight aniseed scent. If too fiery, just reduce the number of dried chillies. This dish would traditionally be served with dosa (crispy lentil pancakes) or appams (rice pancakes), but it is just as good with plain boiled rice.

Serves 4-6

1 tablespoon poppy seeds

1 teaspoon coriander seeds

1 teaspoon cumin seeds

1 teaspoon fennel seeds

3 dried red chillies

1-inch (3 cm) stick of cinnamon

2 cardamom pods

3 cloves

9 tablespoons (50 g) grated coconut

2 garlic cloves, crushed

2 teaspoons grated ginger

2 tablespoons (30 ml) oil

10 curry leaves

2 onions, thinly sliced

1 star anise

2 tomatoes, diced

½ teaspoon turmeric

1 teaspoon chilli powder

salt to taste

8 chicken thighs, skinned

2 limes, cut in halves

handful of fresh coriander leaves, chopped

Gently heat a frying pan on medium to low heat and roast the poppy, coriander, cumin, and fennel seeds; dried red chillies; cinnamon; cardamom; cloves; and coconut for 3 to 4 minutes.

Remove from the heat, transfer to a bowl, and let cool.

Once cooled, grind to a fine powder in a spice grinder.

Crush the garlic and ginger with a mortar and pestle and set aside.

In a large pan, heat the oil on medium heat and add the curry leaves. When they stop sputtering, add the sliced onions and fry until light brown. Add the crushed garlic and ginger.

Add the star anise and fry, then stir in the ground spices for a minute before adding a splash of water.

Add the diced tomatoes, turmeric, chilli powder, and salt. Cook for 10 minutes, allowing the tomatoes to break down.

Add the chicken and stir to coat with the sauce. Cover and simmer on the lowest setting until the chicken is tender, about 25 minutes.

Once the chicken is cooked through, squeeze in the juice from the limes, and remove from the heat.

Sprinkle on the fresh coriander leaves and serve.

Keralan Pork

Pork is not a primary meat for many Indians, but there are some South Indian states where it's considered a delicacy. I think it's a great protein, as it easily carries flavors and works well with spices. Depending on the cut, it can be slow-cooked for a deep, rich curry or you can make a quick, easy meal with loin steaks. It is also a lean meat, once trimmed. Pork and fennel are great friends, and the coconut milk makes a wonderful, velvety masala. Add green beans, baby corn, or red pepper for color and vibrancy.

Serves 4-6

1⅓ to 2 pounds (600 g to 900 g) pork loin steaks or fillets

sea salt to taste

freshly ground black pepper

1 teaspoon ground turmeric (separated)

2 tablespoons (30 ml) coconut oil

1 teaspoon fennel seeds or 2 star anise

2 dried red chillies

2 onions, finely diced

5 garlic cloves, minced

14 ounces (400 g) canned tomatoes

1 tablespoon (15 g) tamarind paste

2 fresh green chillies, chopped

1 tablespoon fresh ginger, grated

2 teaspoons cumin seeds

1 teaspoon coriander seeds

approximately 1 cup (200 g) coconut cream

3½ ounces (100 g) green beans, trimmed

handful of fresh coriander leaves, chopped

Remove the fat from the pork and cut into strips. Season the pork with salt and lots of black pepper and ½ teaspoon of the turmeric.

Heat a wide pan on medium heat and add the oil. Once hot, add the whole fennel seeds and red chillies.

Add the onions and sauté until they start to brown, then add the minced garlic.

Add the canned tomatoes, tamarind paste, green chillies, and grated ginger and stir to combine.

Grind the cumin and coriander with a mortar and pestle.

Once the masala starts to simmer, add the remaining turmeric, and ground cumin and coriander, and stir. Let it reduce and thicken.

Add the pork and stir to coat with the sauce. Reduce the heat and cook for 5 to 10 minutes.

Pour in the coconut cream and heat through. Then add the trimmed beans and cook for an additional 5 minutes until the beans are tender.

When the pork is cooked through, check the seasoning, add the coriander leaves, and serve with plain rice.

Nariyal Chicken

This is a hybrid dish, with a base sauce from the north but using flavors from the south. It is one of my personal favorites because it really packs a punch, yet is quick and easy to make. It works very well with white fish too, if you prefer.

Serves 4-6

1 tablespoon (15 ml) coconut oil

1 teaspoon cumin seeds

2 medium onions, blended in a food processor to a grated consistency

7 ounces (200 g) canned plum tomatoes

1 teaspoon salt

1 teaspoon turmeric

½ teaspoon chilli powder (optional)

2 to 3 green chillies, chopped

approximately 1 cup (200 g) coconut cream

1 pound (500 g) chicken thighs, trimmed and cut into bite-size chunks

1 teaspoon garam masala

handful of fresh coriander leaves, chopped

Heat the coconut oil in a pan until it melts and add the cumin seeds. When sizzling and aromatic, add the onions and fry until a golden color.

Add the tomatoes, salt, turmeric, chilli powder, and fresh chillies. Stir together and cook until the tomatoes break down, leaving a thick paste.

Pour in the coconut cream and cook gently for a few minutes so the flavors combine. Add the chicken, and stir to coat with the sauce.

Reduce the heat to the lowest setting, place the lid half on the pan, and cook for about 10 minutes.

Taste the sauce and adjust the seasoning if required.

Remove from the heat and add the garam masala, and sprinkle on the fresh coriander to serve.

Malabari Prawns

This vibrant curry is all about South Indian coastal flavors, from the prawns to the coconut and curry leaves. The sauce is simply divine—the perfect balance of sweet, salt, bitter, and chilli. If you want to lighten it up, add kokum (a fruit used in South Indian cuisine as a souring agent), tamarind, or a squeeze of lime. I would recommend that you get the biggest, juiciest prawns you can find for this, but you can also use fish.

Serves 4-6

1 tablespoon (15 ml) coconut oil

1 teaspoon fenugreek seeds

5 garlic cloves, sliced

20 curry leaves

3-inch (7 cm) piece of fresh ginger, thinly sliced

2 to 3 green chillies, sliced diagonally

7 shallots, sliced

14 ounces (400 g) canned tomatoes

1 teaspoon salt

1 teaspoon turmeric

1 teaspoon hot red chilli powder

1 teaspoon coriander powder

3 tablespoons coconut powder

approximately ¾ to 1 cup (200 ml) coconut milk

1 pound (500 g) king prawns, cleaned and deveined

handful of fresh coriander leaves, chopped

Heat the oil in a pan over medium heat, add the fenugreek seeds, and stir for a few seconds (you don't want them to darken in color).

Add the sliced garlic and brown it before adding the curry leaves, sliced ginger, and sliced chillies. Stir and cook for 1 to 2 minutes.

Add the shallots and cook until soft and just starting to brown (about 10 minutes).

Using a hand blender or immersion blender, purée the canned tomatoes and add to the pan with the salt. Stir through and cook for a few minutes.

Add the turmeric, red chilli powder, and coriander powder and stir.

In a bowl, mix the coconut powder with some water to make a watery paste, and stir into the masala.

Bring to a boil, then reduce the heat to simmer until it's nice and thick. Add the coconut milk, and mix it together.

Once the sauce is thick and wonderfully rich in color at the desired consistency, check the seasoning and adjust if required. Stir in the raw prawns and cook until they change color.

Remove the pan from the heat, stir in the coriander leaves, and serve with some plain boiled rice.

Tangy Tamarind Prawns

Tamarind is a sour fruit native to India, used to add tang to dishes and chutneys. It's less harsh than lemon, and it enhances depth and color, too. I like to make this fairly spicy, so once I have dished up some for the kids, I add sliced fresh chillies just for me. The sauce is thick and rich, making it perfect to scoop up with poori or naan.

Serves 4-6

2 tablespoons (30 ml) oil

1 teaspoon cumin seeds

1 onion, thinly sliced

2 garlic cloves, finely chopped

7 ounces (200 g) canned tomatoes

1 tablespoon fresh ginger, grated

1 teaspoon turmeric

1 teaspoon salt

1 chilli, finely chopped

1 tablespoon (15 g) tamarind paste (or a good squeeze of lemon juice)

1 pound (500 g) fresh king prawns, cleaned and deveined

GARNISH

2 fresh tomatoes, finely diced

1 teaspoon garam masala

handful of fresh coriander leaves, chopped

2 chillies, sliced (optional)

Heat the oil in a pan over medium heat. Add the cumin seeds; when sizzling, add the onion and garlic. Fry gently until golden brown.

Once browned, reduce the heat and add the canned tomatoes, ginger, turmeric, salt, chilli, and tamarind paste. Increase the heat and stir so the tomatoes and onions melt together, creating a thick masala sauce.

Once the sauce is shiny, add the prawns and stir to coat them with the sauce. Reduce the heat and cook through for a few minutes.

Add the fresh tomatoes, stir and cook for a minute, and then remove from the heat.

Stir in the garam masala, sprinkle on the coriander, top with the chillies (optional), and serve.

Red Lentil Dhal

Daal, dal, dhal—however you spell it, it's just a catchall name for any lentil soup dish. It's a staple part of the Indian diet; in fact, rice and dhal are all many Indians have to eat. It's cheap, nutritious, versatile, and honestly very tasty.

There are many different dhal recipes from different regions. This one is my go-to comfort dish: warm, comforting, a full-on hug in a bowl!

Serves 4-6

7 ounces (200 g) red lentils, washed

1 teaspoon salt

approximately 4 cups (900 ml) water

MASALA

1 tablespoon (15 ml) ghee or rapeseed oil

1 dried red chilli

1 bay leaf

1 teaspoon cumin seeds

1 small onion, chopped

1 garlic clove, chopped

2 tomatoes, finely chopped

1 teaspoon fresh ginger, grated

1 teaspoon turmeric

1 teaspoon fenugreek leaves

1 chilli, finely chopped

1 teaspoon garam masala

handful of fresh coriander leaves, chopped

Place lentils in a pan with the salt, cover with the water, and bring to a boil.

Remove the froth, reduce the heat, and simmer for 10 minutes. Check that the lentils are cooked by squeezing them between your fingers. Once soft, remove them from the heat.

In a frying pan, heat the oil or ghee on medium heat. Add the dried chilli, bay leaf, and cumin seeds.

When the seeds sizzle, add the onion and garlic and fry until lightly browned. Reduce the heat and add the tomatoes, ginger, turmeric, fenugreek leaves, and chopped chilli. Gently let the ingredients cook down for about 10 minutes to make a thick masala paste.

Pour the cooked lentils into the masala—it should have the consistency of a thick soup, but if it's too thick, just add a little boiling water. Or if you prefer it thicker, let it simmer and reduce.

Check the seasoning and add a little salt if required. Stir in the garam masala and coriander to serve.

Rajma

A traditional, wholesome Punjabi dish, rajma is like an Indian vegetarian chili. Use canned kidney beans; if you use dried beans, you will need to soak the beans overnight and cook them in a pressure cooker.

Serves 4-6

1 tablespoon (15 ml) oil

1 small onion, finely diced

4 garlic cloves, finely chopped

7 ounces (200 g) canned plum tomatoes

2 teaspoons fresh ginger, grated

1 chilli, roughly chopped

1 teaspoon turmeric

1 teaspoon salt

14 ounces (400 g) canned kidney beans or 7 ounces (200 g) dried red kidney beans, soaked overnight and cooked in a pressure cooker

1 teaspoon garam masala

handful of fresh coriander leaves, chopped

In a pan, heat the oil on high heat and add the onion and garlic. Fry until brown.

Reduce the heat and stir in the tomatoes, ginger, chilli, turmeric, and salt, and cook for about 5 to 10 minutes to create a thick, shiny masala paste.

Add the cooked or canned kidney beans to the masala paste and stir. Leave on a gentle heat for about 10 minutes, stirring occasionally.

Add the garam masala and chopped coriander to serve.

Vegetable Kofta Curry

Kofta, or meatless meatballs, can be made with any vegetables you have in the fridge. Chickpeas and cooked lentils work too. This recipe includes a creamy cashew nut sauce to put the kofta in, but you can also make them as a nibble or snack with a chutney or dip to dunk them into.

Serves 4-6

VEGETARIAN KOFTA

1 large potato

3 ounces (80 g) cauliflower florets

1½ ounces (40 g) green peas

1½ ounces (40 g) carrots

1½ ounces (40 g) green beans

1½ ounces (40 g) red pepper

1 green chilli

9 ounces (250 g) paneer

handful of fresh coriander leaves

1 teaspoon coriander seeds, crushed

1 teaspoon garam masala

1 teaspoon cumin seeds, crushed

1 teaspoon Kashmiri chilli powder

1 teaspoon mango powder

¼ teaspoon black pepper

1 teaspoon salt

¼ to ½ cup (25 to 50 g) gram flour

oil for frying

MASALA

2 tablespoons cashew nuts

1 onion

4 garlic cloves

3-inch (7 cm) piece of fresh ginger

1 green chilli

1 tablespoon rapeseed oil

1 teaspoon cumin seeds

1 bay leaf

4 green cardamom pods

3-inch (7 cm) piece of cassia bark

1 blade of mace

3 cloves

2 tomatoes or 7 ounces (200 g) canned tomatoes

1 teaspoon coriander seeds

½ teaspoon cumin seeds

1 teaspoon salt

1 teaspoon Kashmiri chilli powder

1 teaspoon turmeric

2 tablespoons (30 g) yogurt

1 teaspoon garam masala

VEGETABLE KOFTA

Add the vegetables—potato, cauliflower florets, green peas, carrots, beans, pepper, and green chilli—and the paneer into a food processor and blitz. Place the mixture into a bowl.

Chop the coriander leaves and add to the bowl along with the spices. Mix it all together.

Sprinkle in the gram flour a little at a time until it starts to bind the vegetables together.

Using one hand, squish everything together until it's thick and you can make balls with the mixture.

Heat the oil for frying the kofta. Test that it's hot enough by adding a little of the mixture—if it sinks, sizzles, and immediately floats back up, then it is ready. If it's too hot, the kofta will brown too quickly and remain raw inside.

Make golf ball–sized balls and very carefully place into the oil. Gently turn them to brown all over, about 3 to 5 minutes. Using a slotted spoon, remove to a dish lined with paper towels. Taste the first one to check that it's cooked inside and the seasoning is correct. If not, adjust the seasoning or return to the oil before cooking the rest. Cook the kofta in batches.

MASALA

Soak the cashews in hot water for around 20 minutes.

Place the onion, garlic, ginger, and chillies in a blender to make a smooth paste.

Heat the oil in a pan over medium heat and add the cumin seeds, bay leaf, green cardamom, cassia bark, mace, and cloves, and fry the spices until fragrant.

Add the onion paste and stir to cook until it starts to brown. If it catches, add a little splash of water and continue to cook. This will take about 20 minutes.

Grind the cashews with a little water to make a smooth paste and set aside.

Once the onions have browned, purée the tomatoes and add to the pan.

Grind the coriander and cumin seeds with a mortar and pestle. Add this and the salt, chilli powder, and turmeric and mix well. Cook until it starts to thicken, and then stir in the cashew paste.

Whip the yogurt with a little water to loosen it up. Stir in the yogurt and mix.

The sauce should be quite thick; add water to the pan to adjust the consistency so it's at a thickness you like.

Simmer for a few minutes, and then stir in the garam masala.

Add the kofta to the masala just before serving and cook for 2 minutes.

Muttar Paneer

This is a real old-school Punjabi dish that plays an important part in the Indian diet, as many Indians are vegetarians. Paneer is also known as Indian cottage cheese. It is an acid-set cheese that is made from cow or buffalo milk. It's made by curdling milk with a fruit or vegetable acid, then pressing the curd until it's a solid block. It can be used as is, diced and fried, or grated and added to curries. The cheese is not aged; it doesn't melt; and it adds texture, much like tofu.

Serves 4-6

enough oil in a small pan to deep-fry the paneer

5 ounces (150 g) paneer, cut into approximately 2-inch (5 cm) cubes

1 tablespoon (15 ml) oil

1 teaspoon cumin seeds

1 onion, finely sliced

3 garlic cloves, sliced

9 ounces (250 g) canned plum tomatoes

1-inch (3 cm) piece of fresh ginger, grated

1 green chilli, finely chopped

1 teaspoon salt

1 teaspoon turmeric

1 teaspoon fenugreek powder (methi)

1 teaspoon Kashmiri chilli powder

7 ounces (200 g) frozen peas

1 teaspoon garam masala

handful of fresh coriander leaves, chopped

Heat enough oil in a pan to deep-fry the paneer over medium to high heat, and gently fry the paneer until golden brown. Remove and set on paper towels.

In another pan, heat more cooking oil and add the cumin seeds until they sizzle.

Add the onion and, after a few minutes, stir in the garlic. Cook for 10 minutes, until the onions are soft and turning golden.

When the onions are golden, add the tomatoes, ginger, chilli, salt, turmeric, fenugreek powder, and chilli powder. Using your stirring spoon, squish the tomatoes to break them down. Stir, and let the masala come together, about 10 minutes, until it becomes thick and shiny.

Once it's thick, add the fried paneer and frozen peas. Stir and cook for 2 to 3 minutes.

Pour in enough hot water to cover the paneer, and simmer for 10 minutes.

Remove from the heat, and sprinkle in the garam masala and fresh coriander to serve.

Cabbage Thoran

Vegetarian Indian food is just delightful. We are not afraid to add big, bold flavors to delicate vegetables. "Thoran" is a generic term used for a dry vegetable curry in Kerala that can literally be made with any of the local, seasonal vegetables. Keralan cuisine is known for lots of green vegetables—snake beans, tindori, ivy berries, and unripe jackfruit are common, as well as leafy greens. So feel free to try different vegetables with this recipe.

Serves 4-6

3 tablespoons (45 ml) coconut oil

2 teaspoons black mustard seeds

2 tablespoons chopped, fresh curry leaves

1 teaspoon cumin seeds

2 dried Kashmiri chillies, each broken into smaller pieces

2-inch (5 cm) piece of fresh ginger, finely grated

½ teaspoon turmeric

1 teaspoon salt

½ teaspoon ground black pepper

9 ounces (250 g) white cabbage, shredded

2 fresh green chillies, sliced

3½ ounces (100 g) fresh coconut, grated

Heat the oil on medium heat in a large saucepan or karahi. When it is hot, add the mustard seeds followed by the curry leaves, cumin seeds, and dried chillies.

Stir for about 30 seconds, then add the grated ginger, turmeric, salt, and black pepper, and fry for 30 seconds.

Stir in the cabbage and cook over medium heat for 5 to 7 minutes. (You may need to add a splash of water.)

Once the cabbage is tender, stir in the green chillies and coconut. Heat through for a few minutes and serve. Perfect with some fresh boiled rice.

Aloo Gobi

I was about seven or eight years old when my mum and dad had to unexpectedly fly back to India, leaving us to stay with a family friend. After a week of indulging in 1980s-era English meals (something we didn't have often, so it was a real novelty), we all started to crave my mum's food. So my sister and I decided to cook aloo gobi. Nervous about getting it wrong, we phoned my aunt to ask if we could cook the cauliflower in one giant lump, or did we need to cut it into pieces? She still laughs when she tells that story. Needless to say, our version wasn't as good as my mum's, but this recipe absolutely makes up for that. And the robust tomato sauce is very special; if you can hold your nerve and not add water, it will be cooked to perfection.

Serves 4-6

1 small cauliflower
2 tablespoons (30 ml) mustard oil
1 teaspoon mustard seeds
1 teaspoon cumin seeds
1 onion, finely chopped
2 garlic cloves, finely chopped
7 ounces (200 g) canned tomatoes
1 tablespoon fresh ginger, grated
1 teaspoon salt
1 teaspoon turmeric
1 chilli, finely chopped
1 teaspoon dried fenugreek leaves
2 potatoes, peeled and cut into
    1½-inch (4 cm) cubes
1 teaspoon garam masala
handful of fresh coriander leaves,
    chopped

Prepare your cauliflower by cutting into florets; wash and drain. Ensure it's thoroughly dry before cooking.

Heat the oil on medium heat in a large saucepan or karahi and add the mustard seeds. Once sizzling, add the cumin seeds.

Add the onions and garlic and fry until soft and lightly browned.

Once browned, reduce the heat a little and add the tomatoes, ginger, salt, turmeric, chilli, and dried fenugreek leaves.

Continue to cook so the onions and tomatoes melt together to create a thick, aromatic masala paste.

Add the potatoes and stir to coat with the sauce.

Reduce the heat, cover the pan with a lid, and cook for 10 minutes, stirring occasionally.

Add the cauliflower and stir into the sauce to coat. Replace the lid and cook for an additional 25 to 30 minutes. Turn the vegetables occasionally, but do not stir too vigorously as you don't want the cauliflower or potato to turn mushy.

Once cooked, sprinkle with the garam masala and fresh coriander before serving.

Top Tip • This dish can also be baked, if you prefer. After you add the cauliflower, pour everything into an oven tray, place in a hot oven at 350°F (180°C, or gas mark 4), and bake for 20 minutes.

Spiced Mushroom Pilau

One-pot dishes are perfect for family dinners, and although this may look like a long list of ingredients, it's actually pretty simple to make. I know my kids aren't mushroom fans—apparently it's a texture thing—so you can substitute them for chicken or cauliflower if you prefer.

Serves 4-6

7 ounces (200 g) basmati rice

MUSHROOM MASALA

2 to 3 tablespoons (30 to 45 ml) oil

1 teaspoon fennel seeds

1 teaspoon cumin seeds

1-inch (3 cm) piece of cassia bark

2 cloves

3 green cardamom pods

2 blades of mace

1 bay leaf

1 star anise

10 curry leaves

1 onion, finely chopped

6 garlic cloves, minced

3-inch (7 cm) piece of fresh ginger, minced

1 or 2 green chillies, finely chopped

1 tomato, finely chopped

1 teaspoon coriander powder

1 teaspoon turmeric powder

1 teaspoon red chilli powder

½ teaspoon garam masala powder

¼ teaspoon black pepper

1 teaspoon salt

9 ounces (250 g) chestnut mushrooms, cut into chunks

handful of fresh mint leaves, chopped

handful of fresh coriander leaves, chopped

Rinse the basmati rice in running water till the water runs clear of starch. Soak the rice in enough water to cover it and leave for 30 minutes. Then, drain the rice and set aside.

MUSHROOM MASALA

Heat the oil in a deep pan over medium heat, then add all the whole spices—fennel, cumin, cassia, cloves, green cardamom, mace, bay leaf, and star anise.

Stir in the curry leaves and fry the spices until fragrant for a few seconds, and then add chopped onions and sauté until they are translucent.

Add the minced garlic, minced ginger, and green chillies and cook until the garlic is lightly browned.

Add the chopped tomato and sauté for about 10 minutes.

Add the coriander powder, turmeric powder, red chilli powder, garam masala powder, black pepper, and salt.

Once fragrant and the tomatoes have broken down into the masala, add the mushrooms and half the mint and coriander leaves. Cook on low heat for 6 to 8 minutes.

Stir and add almost 1 cup (200 ml) of hot water. Bring the mixture to a simmer.

Add the rice and the remaining mint and coriander and stir through. Season with salt.

Reduce the heat and cover the pan with a lid. Cook for 10 minutes.

Once the water has been absorbed, check that the rice is cooked. If it still has a bite, add a little more water and cook with the lid on for a little longer.

Once the rice is cooked through, remove from the heat and let rest with the lid on for 5 minutes.

Remove the lid and fluff the rice before serving.

Chilli Paneer

India is a nation that not only exports its own flavors but also readily absorbs those of its neighbors. Indo-Chinese food is very popular in India, everywhere from roadside carts to markets to the very poshest restaurants. These recipes have pulled in typically Chinese ingredients such as noodles and soy sauce and combined them with paneer, spices, and masala. Prepared using Chinese cooking styles but with a very Indian flair, these dishes are perfect for the international palate.

Serves 4-6

14 ounces (400 g) paneer, chopped into cubes

oil for frying

PANEER BATTER

3 tablespoons (23 g) plain flour

1 tablespoon corn flour

1 teaspoon Kashmiri chilli powder

salt to taste

2 to 3 tablespoons (30 to 45 ml) water

CHILLI SAUCE

3 to 4 Kashmiri chillies, soaked in hot water

1-inch (3 cm) piece of fresh ginger, roughly chopped

2 tablespoons (30 ml) rapeseed oil

1 teaspoon cumin seeds

4 garlic cloves, finely chopped

1 red onion, chopped into cubes

1 red pepper, chopped into cubes

1 green chilli, slit lengthwise

1 tablespoon (15 ml) soy sauce

sea salt to taste (if required)

2 spring or green onions, finely sliced for garnish

large pinch of fresh coriander leaves, chopped

PANEER BATTER

In a small pan, heat some oil on medium to high heat in which to deep-fry the paneer.

Place all the ingredients for the batter into a bowl to make a thick batter, adding more water if needed.

Place the paneer cubes into the batter to coat them completely. Once the oil is hot (check by dropping in a little batter—if it sinks, and then immediately rises, it's ready). Fry the paneer until the cubes are golden brown and crisp. Remove with a slotted spoon, drain on paper towels, and set aside.

CHILLI SAUCE

Blend the soaked chillies with the fresh ginger to make a paste.

Heat the oil in a pan on medium heat and stir in the cumin seeds until fragrant.

Add the garlic and sauté until it just starts to color (be careful it doesn't burn).

Scrape in the chilli and ginger paste and cook for a minute until the oil separates. Add the red onion and cook for a few minutes to soften, then add the red pepper and sliced chilli.

Stir in the soy sauce and a tiny splash of water if required.

Stir in the fried paneer so it's all coated in the sauce.

Check the seasoning and adjust as needed. Top with spring onions and chopped coriander. Serve with spiced noodles or rice.

Top Tip • Make it vegan by simply replacing the paneer with tofu or soya. You can use sriracha chilli sauce instead of making it yourself.

Chana Masala with Spinach

Chickpeas in a hearty tomato masala with the addition of spinach or kale makes a wonderful meat-free midweek meal that's quick and nutritious.

Serves 4–6

- 1 to 2 tablespoons (15 to 30 ml) rapeseed oil
- ½ teaspoon mustard seeds
- 1 teaspoon cumin seeds
- 1 large onion, diced
- 4 garlic cloves, crushed
- 4 plum tomatoes or 7 ounces (200 g) canned tomatoes
- 1 heaped teaspoon coriander seeds, crushed
- 1 green chilli, chopped
- 1 teaspoon red chilli powder
- 1 teaspoon turmeric
- 1 teaspoon salt, or to taste
- 28 ounces (800 g) (2 14-ounce cans) chickpeas, drained and rinsed
- 7 ounces (200 g) spinach or kale, roughly chopped
- 1 green chilli, sliced for garnish

Heat the oil in a lidded pan over medium heat, and add the mustard and cumin seeds.

Stir for a minute until you can smell the aroma of the mustard and cumin seeds; when they stop sizzling, add the diced onions.

Fry the onions for 15 minutes until they start to brown, then add the garlic. Fry together for 4 minutes before adding the tomatoes. Stir and cook for a few minutes. Add a little water if required.

Add the crushed coriander, green chilli, chilli powder, turmeric, and salt. Cook on a gentle heat until the tomatoes start to break down and create a thick masala sauce (about 10 minutes).

Turn the heat up to thicken the sauce a little if required. Add the chickpeas and stir to coat them with the masala. Add a splash of water and let them simmer for 5 minutes.

Add the chopped spinach, a handful at a time, stirring in between. Remove from the heat and allow the spinach to wilt through the dish.

Top with the sliced chilli and serve with poori and fresh plain yogurt.

Top Tip • If your kids are a bit anti-veg, remove their portion before adding the spinach to the dish. They will love scooping this up with the poori.

Pineapple Curry

I know what you're thinking—it's a weird one! But I personally love this South Indian specialty. Coastal flavors, creamy coconut, hot chillies, zingy pineapple—what's not to love? Plus, it cooks down to a wonderful meaty texture, yet it's totally vegan!

Serves 4-6

1 tablespoon (15 ml) coconut oil

1 teaspoon mustard seeds

4 cardamom pods

¾-inch (2 cm) piece of cassia bark

1 onion, diced

4 garlic cloves, minced

1-inch (3 cm) piece of fresh ginger, grated

1 red chilli, sliced

1 teaspoon turmeric

1 teaspoon lemon pepper, crushed (or just black pepper)

½ teaspoon chilli powder

½ teaspoon salt, or to taste

1 pineapple, peeled, cored, and diced

1¾ cups (400 ml) coconut milk

Heat the coconut oil in a pan over medium heat and add the mustard seeds, cardamom, and cassia bark until the seeds pop.

Add the diced onion and stir until translucent.

Add the garlic and cook for about 5 minutes.

As the onions just start to brown, add the ginger, chilli, turmeric, pepper, chilli powder, and salt, and stir.

Add the pineapple pieces and coat with the masala spices.

Pour in the coconut milk and turn up the heat to bring to a simmer.

Put the lid on and simmer gently for 30 minutes or until you are happy with how much the pineapple has softened—I prefer mine soft.

Turmeric & Honey Bread

Making bread interesting with the use of spices is so much fun, allowing you to get creative and try new things. This recipe was created to dunk into a heart-warming soup. Once you start baking your own bread, it's hard to go back to the store-bought stuff. I have used atta here, but you can use a strong bread flour as well.

Serves 4-6

1¾ teaspoons (7 g) yeast
5 tablespoons (75 ml) warm water
½ teaspoon sugar
3⅓ cups (400 g) atta
2 tablespoons (30 g) yogurt
2 tablespoons (30 ml) ghee
2 tablespoons (30 g) honey
1 teaspoon salt
2 teaspoons kalonji seeds
2 teaspoons turmeric
approximately ¾ cup
    (150 to 200 ml) water

In a small bowl, combine the yeast, warm water, and sugar, and stir. Let sit for 5 to 10 minutes until frothy.

Place all the other ingredients into a bowl except the water.

Pour in the yeast and slowly add the water a little at a time. The amount of water needed can vary depending on the flour, so be careful.

Knead the dough until it comes together and is soft. Or you can use a mixer with a dough hook to do the same job.

Place the dough in an oiled bowl and cover for 1 hour with a clean, wet tea towel. Leave it in a warm place for it to rise.

Once it has doubled in size, knock it back and knead for a minute or so.

Oil a baking tray, shape the dough into a dome shape, and place on the tray.

Cover again with the tea towel and leave for another hour in a warm place.

Preheat the oven to 400°F (200°C, or gas mark 6) and, once the dough has again doubled in size, bake in the oven for 20 to 25 minutes.

Once it turns a golden color, remove from the oven. When you tap the bottom, it should sound hollow. Leave it on a cooling rack until completely cooled.

Top Tip • If you find you have made the dough too wet, just add more dry flour until you have a nice, soft dough.

Chilla Pancakes

These little green Indian pancakes are a great side bread if you are gluten intolerant, or they make a light, healthy breakfast. They are made with mung beans, which are a light, healthy lentil used for so many different dishes. Light and easy to digest, they taste fantastic. The lentils need to be soaked so they are soft before being blitzed to make a batter, so ensure you give yourself plenty of time to prepare.

Makes 8-10

3½ ounces (100 g) moong dhal (mung beans), whole or split with husk

½ small onion, chopped

1 teaspoon fresh ginger, grated

1 teaspoon fresh coriander leaves, chopped

salt to taste

1 green chilli, chopped

2 to 3 tablespoons (30 to 45 ml) water

1 ounce (30 g) green peas or a handful of spinach (optional)

1 teaspoon baking soda

1 tablespoon (15 ml) ghee or oil, to cook

Soak the moong dhal (mung beans) for 4 hours in a cup of water.

Blitz in a blender with the onion, ginger, coriander, salt, and chilli. Add a little more water to make a thick paste. If using green peas or spinach, blanch in hot water, drain, and add to the blender.

Only when you are ready to cook, add the baking soda and mix everything together. It should be the consistency of thick pancake batter. Add more water if required.

Heat a frying pan or a small egg frying pan to high, then reduce the heat. Add a teaspoon of ghee or oil to coat the pan. Pour in a ladle full of the batter and spread around the pan with the back of a spoon.

Cook for a few minutes. When the top is dry, drizzle on a little more oil and flip it over to cook the other side. They are very delicate, so cook gently (4 to 5 minutes).

Repeat with the remaining mixture and serve hot. They turn quite dark in color, so don't be too surprised!

Spruced-Up Cauliflower Rice

Rice is the basic staple when it comes to Indian food, but if you prefer something less carb heavy, there are other options: brown rice, couscous, polenta, or this lovely cauliflower rice. Much lighter than rice as a side, it becomes a dish in its own right by infusing loads of aromatics into it. This also works as a superb meal to take to work in your lunch box.

Serves 4

1 medium cauliflower

1 tablespoon (15 ml) rapeseed oil

1 teaspoon black mustard seeds

1 teaspoon cumin seeds

2 dried Kashmiri chillies,
   each broken into 3 or 4 pieces

1 garlic clove, sliced

2-inch (5 cm) piece of fresh ginger,
   finely grated

½ teaspoon turmeric

1 teaspoon salt

2 fresh green chillies, sliced

Roughly chop your cauliflower, put into a blender, and blitz very quickly to get a fine shred of cauliflower.

Heat the oil on medium heat in a large saucepan or karahi. When it is hot, add the mustard seeds, followed by the cumin seeds and dried chillies.

Stir for about 30 seconds, and then add the sliced garlic, grated ginger, turmeric, and salt. Fry for 30 seconds.

Stir in the cauliflower rice and stir-fry for about 3 to 4 minutes over medium heat. Stir in the green chillies.

7

Clever Condiments

Why clever, you ask? Well, a good condiment is a sauce or dip that tastes delicious, but a clever condiment is exceptional because it can be used in a variety of ways for a variety of dishes. In this chapter, I offer a selection of accoutrements that are designed to tantalize your taste buds through a number of different mechanisms. Visually, they add vibrancy; by heating and cooling, they add contrast; and with their chunky, crispy, and smooth textures, they add interest. They are just that special.

Mint Chutney

My mum's fresh mint chutney is just the best. Simple to make, yet gives that perfect burst of flavor that will keep you coming back.

Makes 1 cup (250 g)

1 or 2 lemons

large bunch of fresh mint leaves

1 green chilli (add more for more heat)

1 onion, cut into chunks

1 teaspoon salt

Slice the lemon in half and slice off the rind, remove any seeds, and chop the flesh into quarters.

Remove the leaves from the mint, discarding the stalks, and remove the chilli stem too.

Place the lemon, mint, chilli, onion, and salt into a blender and blitz until you get a fine blended chutney.

Top Tip • Add 1 tablespoon of this chutney to 1 cup (250 g) of yogurt just before serving to make a quick raita.

Indian Tomato Ketchup

Once you make this, you'll never reach for the Heinz bottle again. This sweet, tangy sauce not only works on a bacon sandwich but makes a great addition to a cheese board. Seriously easy to make, too.

Makes 3 cups (800 g)

¾ to 1 cup (200 ml) white vinegar

1⅓ cups (250 g) jaggery or
brown sugar

3 tablespoons (45 ml) vegetable oil

1 teaspoon kalonji seeds

1 teaspoon fennel seeds

1 teaspoon mustard seeds

1 teaspoon cumin seeds

½ teaspoon fenugreek seeds

2 dried Kashmiri red chillies

1 red chilli, chopped

2¼ pounds (1 kg) tomatoes,
quartered

1 teaspoon salt, or to taste

1 teaspoon chilli powder (optional)

Dissolve the sugar with the vinegar in a bowl.

Heat the oil over medium heat in a heavy pan and add the kalonji, fennel, mustard, cumin, and fenugreek seeds as well as the chillies. Cook until they sizzle and become fragrant. This should only take a minute.

Very gently, pour the vinegar and sugar mixture into the pan with the spices and stir. Bring this to a simmer.

Add in the tomatoes and cook on a very low heat until they have softened and have gone pulpy (about 45 minutes to 1 hour).

Season with salt and chilli powder, stirring to keep it from sticking. If you want to remove any of the tomato skins, do so with some tongs. Put the ketchup into a sterilized glass jar and cool.

Once cooled, seal the jar. The ketchup will keep for 4 to 6 weeks; refrigerate once opened.

Punjabi Pickled Piyaz

This classic pickled onion side can work as a chutney or a salad. The onions remain crisp but have an added tang to them. Perfect with tandoori chicken or a meaty curry.

Makes 1-1½ cups (250-300 g)

2 red onions, thinly sliced in rings

large pinch of fresh coriander leaves, chopped

1 green chilli, chopped

1 lemon, cut in half

1 teaspoon Kashmiri chilli powder

salt to taste

chaat masala (optional)

Place the sliced onions in a bowl.

Add the chopped coriander and chopped chilli.

Squeeze in the juice from the lemon.

Add the chilli powder, salt, and chaat masala (if using).

Using your hands, mix everything together and serve or store in a sealed container for 2 to 3 days.

Top Tip • If you don't like the strong flavor of onions, slice them and soak them in cold, salted water first.

Mango Chutney

Mango chutney is a very popular dressing in the United Kingdom, especially for poppadoms (Indian lentil crisps). This recipe is a little different from what Americans are used to—it's chunky, made with real mangoes, and has a spicy kick. If you prefer a sweeter, jam-like version, increase the sugar, reduce the chilli, and cook the chutney for longer.

Makes ¾ cup (200 g)

3 tablespoons (45 ml) vegetable oil

1 teaspoon cumin seeds

8 cardamom pods (you can use the seeds only and discard the husks)

3 cloves

1 teaspoon kalonji seeds

5 garlic cloves, crushed

1-inch (3 cm) piece of fresh ginger, peeled and grated

5 to 6 ripe green mangoes, each approximately 9 to 11 ounces (250 to 300 g), peeled, pitted, and diced

1 teaspoon red chilli flakes

1 teaspoon Kashmiri chilli powder

½ teaspoon turmeric powder

½ teaspoon ginger powder

¾ to 1⅓ cups (150 to 250 g) jaggery or brown sugar (I used 150 g)

2 teaspoons salt flakes

1 cup (250 ml) cider vinegar

2 red chillies, sliced (increase for more kick)

Heat the oil in a large pan over medium heat and add the cumin, cardamom, and cloves for a few seconds until they become aromatic.

Add the kalonji seeds. Add the garlic and ginger and stir for a few seconds.

Add the diced mango pieces with the chilli flakes, chilli powder, turmeric, ginger powder, brown sugar, salt, and cider vinegar, and stir until the sugar dissolves.

Bring to a boil, and then reduce to a simmer, cooking gently for about 40 to 50 minutes or until the mixture looks syrupy, stirring regularly.

In the meantime, sterilize jars in the oven at 350°F (180°C, or gas mark 4) for 30 minutes.

Stir in the chopped red chillies 20 minutes before the end of cooking.

Put the chutney into hot sterilized jars and immediately seal with lids. Once you open the jar, store in the fridge and use within 4 weeks.

Coconut & Chilli Chutney

This South Indian–style chutney is wonderful; it uses a technique popular in the region. By toasting lentils the same way you would toast spices, it adds a unique texture and bite. This recipe reminds me of sitting in a hotel dining room in India with the biggest breakfast dosa in front of me: sambar (a lentil and vegetable dish) and coconut chutney. Pure happiness!

Makes ¾ cup (200 g)

2 tablespoons chana dhal (yellow lentils)

CHUTNEY

½ cup fresh coconut, grated or roughly chopped

½ teaspoon cumin powder

1 to 2 green chillies

1 garlic clove

water as needed

salt, to taste

TADKA

¾ tablespoon coconut oil

¼ teaspoon brown mustard seeds

½ to ¾ teaspoon urad dhal (black lentils)

1 dried red chilli, broken

5 to 8 curry leaves

¼ teaspoon asafoetida

Heat a small pan over high heat and add the chana dhal. Dry-roast it until it turns a golden color. Remove and let cool.

Blend all the ingredients for the chutney in a blender. You will likely need to scrape the sides down, add a little water, and run it again to create a grainy but blended mixture.

Stir in the salt to taste (about ½ teaspoon).

Heat a tadka pan or other small pan and add coconut oil, mustard seeds, urad dhal, and red chilli. Sauté until golden in color (see page 13).

Add the curry leaves and asafoetida and remove from the heat.

Once the leaves turn crisp, pour the tadka over the coconut chutney and serve.

Indian Chimichurri

Chimichurri is a popular Argentinian condiment that is freshly made and used to baste grilled meat at most dinner tables. It's great with both chicken and red meats, especially steak, and it's an easy way to freshen up barbecued meats—just drizzle a few tablespoons over the meat once it's cooked.

I realized how similar chimichurri is to the chutneys we use in Indian food—always freshly made with fragrant herbs, with a chilli kick and an acidity, usually from lemons or limes. Classic chimichurri uses wine vinegar, oregano, and parsley. I substituted some popular Indian ingredients, and it works really well both in taste and vibrancy with Indian marinated meats.

Makes 1 cup (200 g)

2 tablespoons (30 ml) lemon juice

handful of fresh coriander leaves, finely chopped

pinch of fresh mint, chopped

3 garlic cloves, minced

2 small red chillies, finely chopped

1 teaspoon cumin seeds, toasted and crushed

1 teaspoon rock salt

black pepper, to taste

½ cup (140 ml) rapeseed oil

Put all the ingredients except the oil into a small bowl and mix. Pour in the oil and stir. Let sit for 10 minutes.

Drizzle over grilled meats and fish.

Store in the refrigerator for 24 hours. Give it a good mix before serving.

Pomegranate Raita

You always need the refreshing, cooling element of yogurt. Yogurt is so versatile that it's a great base for something extravagant. When flavored, it becomes a raita. You can use anything—beetroot, cucumber, spices, mint. This one is a little unusual, but it works so beautifully. When eaten, the little pomegranate gems pop, with a zingy, fruity tang I love!

Makes ¾ cup (250 g)

1 cup (250 g) Greek yogurt
½ teaspoon cumin seeds
1 teaspoon jaggery or brown sugar
2 tablespoons (18 g) pomegranate seeds
2 tablespoons grated cucumber
½ teaspoon salt

Put the yogurt into a bowl and beat it a little to aerate.

Toast the cumin seeds in a frying pan until fragrant, then add to the yogurt.

Add all the other ingredients and stir through.

Mango Kachumber

Kachumber is a finely diced salad made with lots of different ingredients. It's great to scoop up with chips or serve as a side with kebabs.

Makes 1¼ cups (250 g)

1 red onion, very finely diced
handful of fresh coriander leaves, chopped
½ red chilli, finely chopped
juice of 1 lime
1 large ripe mango, peeled, pitted, and finely diced
½ teaspoon kalonji seeds

Combine the onion, coriander, and chilli in a bowl.

Add the lime juice, diced mango, and kalonji seeds. Stir, and let sit for 10 minutes. Stir again and serve.

Avocado & Spinach Yogurt

I can't begin to tell you how good this is: vibrant to look at, smooth and creamy and refreshing beyond belief, but still with a kick. It's great as a dip but even better for breakfast!

Makes 1-1¼ cups (250-300 g)

1 ripe avocado, cut in half and pitted

1 green chilli

handful of fresh coriander (including stalks)

big handful of baby spinach

1 cup (250 g) Greek yogurt

juice of half 1 lemon

1 teaspoon cumin seeds

1 teaspoon salt

Scoop out the avocado flesh and place it in a blender.

Add all the remaining ingredients and blend until nice and smooth.

Check the seasoning, and adjust if required.

Indian Slaw

Coleslaw, traditionally a dish of cabbage, vinegar, eggs, and spices, dates back to Roman times. It's a common side to Caribbean dishes in much the same way that raita is served with Indian curries. I developed this dish to add a little twist, and wow, people went crazy for it! Shredded cabbage, red onions, and a few cumin seeds are all wrapped up in a creamy mix of yogurt and mayonnaise with a cashew crunch that comes together deliciously fresh and fragrant. There is nothing more satisfying than making your own coleslaw, because the store-bought versions will never compare.

Makes 2½ cups (500 g)

2 to 3 medium carrots, peeled and coarsely shredded

½ white cabbage, cored and finely shredded

1 red onion, halved and finely sliced

½ teaspoon cumin seeds, toasted

1½ ounces (40 g) cashews

3 tablespoons (45 g) Greek yogurt

2 tablespoons (28 g) mayonnaise

juice of ½ lemon

½ to 1 red chilli (or to taste), finely sliced

1 teaspoon turmeric

½ teaspoon Kashmiri chilli powder

½ teaspoon salt (or to taste)

handful of fresh coriander leaves, chopped

In a large bowl, mix the carrots, cabbage, and onion.

Toast the cumin seeds in a dry pan over high heat until aromatic, and set aside.

Toast the cashew nuts until golden, and set aside.

Mix the toasted cumin seeds, yogurt, mayonnaise, lemon juice, sliced chilli, turmeric, chilli powder, and salt. Tip the yogurt mixture into the shredded veg mix. Stir to mix everything together.

Stir in half the coriander and half the cashews. Sprinkle with remaining coriander and cashews just before serving.

8

Decadent Desserts & Nighttime Treats

What follows are (in my humble opinion) some of the best puddings to have after an Indian meal. These are not the usual super sweet Indian desserts (though I have a place in my heart for those as well!) but just as refreshing, decadent, and, best of all, easy to make.

Vanilla Bhapa Doi

The only way to describe this is a steamed milk pudding—sounds terrible, I know, but I assure you it's amazing. In its original form, it's a classic Bengali dessert made by reducing milk until it's sweet, rich, and creamy. It's then flavored with cardamom and saffron for a golden hue and steamed to perfection, resulting in a set cream similar to a panna cotta. My version is simplified, using only three ingredients and vanilla to flavor it. This unique dessert has a slight yogurty tang, but it's light and served cold, making it perfect after a warming Indian meal. I love to serve with a tangy raspberry sauce for a fruity twist that cuts right through the sweetness.

Makes 6

⅓ cup (100 g) sweetened condensed milk

⅓ cup (100 g) Greek yogurt

½ cup (100 ml) double cream or heavy cream

seeds from 1 vanilla pod

RASPBERRY SAUCE

7 ounces (200 g) raspberries (frozen or fresh)

2 tablespoons (30 ml) water

1 tablespoon (13 g) sugar

½ lime

Preheat the oven to 212°F (100°C).

Whisk all the ingredients in a large glass bowl.

Pour into individual ramekins and place them into a roasting tray. Fill the tray with water until it comes half up the sides of the ramekins.

Cover the tray with plastic wrap.

Very carefully place the tray in the oven to steam for about 25 minutes, or until set. When ready, they should have the consistency of panna cotta.

Remove the plastic wrap and cool. Refrigerate for a few hours before serving.

RASPBERRY SAUCE

Empty the raspberries into a pan with the water, sugar, and a squeeze of lime.

Cook on a gentle heat for about 10 minutes until the fruit has broken down and the sugar has dissolved.

Push the fruit through a fine sieve or strainer to remove the seeds.

Pour over the bhapa doi just before serving.

Top Tip • This dish can be flavored with 1 teaspoon rose water, ½ teaspoon cinnamon, or ¼ teaspoon cardamom powder, or you can even sprinkle caster sugar on top and blowtorch it to make Indian crème brulée!

Cinnamon Chocolate Torte

Everyone loves chocolate torte, and it's even better with a subtle infusion of spice. I have made this torte with chai spices and chilli, but this time I have used cinnamon and pomegranate. These two ingredients are uniquely matched and perfect for an indulgent dessert that's a total crowd-pleaser.

Serves 6-8

BISCUIT CRUST

6 ounces (175 g) digestive biscuits

⅓ cup (85 g) unsalted butter, melted

CINNAMON-INFUSED GANACHE

12 ounces (340 g) good-quality dark chocolate (70 percent cocoa solids), roughly chopped

1 cup (240 ml) double cream or heavy cream

1 stick cinnamon

¼ cup (55 g) butter, cut into small pieces

GARNISH

½ cup (50 g) cocoa powder or confectioners' sugar for dusting

¾ to 1 cup (200 ml) double cream or heavy cream, whipped

1 fresh pomegranate, seeds removed

BISCUIT CRUST

Crush the digestive biscuits. You can either put them in a zip-top bag and crush with a rolling pin, or put them in a food processor and finely grind until broken down.

Transfer the crumbs to a medium bowl and pour in the melted butter. Mix until they are fully combined.

Press the mixture onto the bottom and up the sides of a 9-inch (23 cm) tart pan.

Place in the fridge for 30 minutes to firm up, or bake the crust at 350°F (180°C, or gas mark 4) for 5 minutes. Cool completely.

CINNAMON-INFUSED GANACHE

In a heatproof bowl, place chopped dark chocolate and set aside.

Pour the cream into a small saucepan and add the cinnamon stick. Simmer gently over medium heat to infuse.

Add the butter to the cream and bring to a low boil. Remove from the heat and leave to infuse for 30 minutes.

Return to the heat and boil. Then remove the cinnamon stick and pour the infused cream over the chopped chocolate.

Let stand for 1 minute, and then stir the mixture until all the chocolate melts and turns shiny and smooth.

Pour the chocolate mixture over the chilled crust and refrigerate until it sets (at least 4 hours).

Dust with cocoa powder or confectioners' sugar and serve with whipped cream and a scattering of pomegranate seeds.

Top Tip • Cut the tart with a hot knife to get that perfect slice!

Chilli Chocolate Pots

I made these dessert pots for one of my first events, and I knew I had a winner when I caught some of the guests stealing handfuls of the pots to take home.

Chilli chocolate is less about heat than about the subtle chilli flavor elevating the chocolate. Oh, and the splash of brandy is my favorite touch!

Makes 4-6

1 dried red chilli (plus a pinch of chilli flakes for more heat)

1¼ cups (285 ml) single cream

7 ounces (200 g) dark chocolate (minimum 70 percent cocoa solids)

2 egg yolks, whisked

1 tablespoon (15 ml) brandy

1½ tablespoons (21 g) unsalted butter, softened

Place the chilli and cream into a small, heavy-based pan and heat until the mixture is just about to come to a boil. Take off the heat; then remove and discard the chilli.

Break the chocolate into pieces and add to the hot cream, stirring until melted and smooth.

Allow to cool, then add the whisked egg yolks, brandy, and butter and lightly whisk to combine with chocolate mixture.

Pour the mixture into four small cups and chill in the fridge for 2 to 3 hours before serving.

Top Tip • You can use chilli-flavored chocolate to make this if it seems too complicated to do the infusion yourself. You can also flavor with salt, cinnamon, or honeycomb for variations on the theme.

Vegan Eton Mess

As you may know, Eton mess is a very English, very summery dessert, and this one has a few Indian hints to it: There's rose water in the strawberries, and the cream is whipped coconut milk. But more importantly, it's totally vegan! The meringues are made without eggs, using chickpea water (also known as aquafaba or "bean water"). The starchy water has amazing qualities—when whipped, it produces a light foam just like egg whites. You can add stabilizers such as sugar or cream of tartar to this foam so it doesn't collapse. The same technique can be used to veganize a number of dishes (including mayonnaise).

Serves 4

AQUAFABA MERINGUES

14 ounces (400 g) canned chickpeas

½ cup (110 g) caster sugar

⅛ teaspoon cream of tartar

COCONUT CREAM

14-ounce (400 ml) can full-fat, unsweetened coconut milk (refrigerated overnight)

3 tablespoons (23.5 g) confectioners' sugar

FRUIT

1 pound (500 g) raspberries, strawberries, mixed berries, or any fruit you like

2 teaspoons rose water

AQUAFABA MERINGUES

Drain the canned chickpeas, saving the water (aquafaba).

Preheat the oven to 265°F (130°C, or gas mark 1) and line two baking sheets with parchment paper.

Whisk the aquafaba in a stand mixer fitted with the whisk attachment at high speed for at least 20 minutes until you get stiff white peaks.

Add the sugar to the aquafaba one tablespoon at a time and whisk well after each addition until the sugar granules dissolve. The meringue mixture should turn thick and become glossy when it's ready.

Put spoonfuls of the meringue mixture onto the lined baking sheets, leaving spaces between them. You can also put it into a piping bag and pipe the meringues.

Put the trays in the oven and bake for 1 hour 45 minutes to 2 hours, until the meringues are fairly firm on top and on the base.

When ready, either remove from the oven and cool completely or switch off the oven and leave them to cool before removing them from the parchment paper. Once cooled, they should be light and crisp.

COCONUT CREAM

The can of coconut milk should be refrigerated overnight so that the cream solidifies and separates from the water.

Flip the can over and open it so it is easier to pour the coconut water off. Scrape the coconut cream into a bowl.

Sift in the confectioners' sugar and whisk together until it's soft and creamy.

FRUIT

Mix the berries and rose water together and steep for 15 to 20 minutes.

MAKE THE MESS

Crush the meringues and pop into a glass. Top with cream and berries, add some more meringue and more cream—and serve!

Chocolate & Cardamom Balls

Balls made of chocolate—what else is there to say? If your guests don't like these, perhaps you need to find new guests.

Makes 12-15

9 ounces (250 g) good-quality dark chocolate (70 percent cocoa solids)

½ cup (125 ml) double cream or heavy cream

2 tablespoons (28 g) butter

¼ teaspoon cardamom powder

1 pinch sea salt

½ cup (50 g) good-quality cocoa powder

cinnamon powder, for dusting

Break up the chocolate and place in a small bowl.

In a saucepan, heat the cream to just boiling before removing from the heat and adding the butter.

Pour the hot cream over the chocolate and add the cardamom powder and salt.

Stir to melt the chocolate; let it rest and stir again. Once it has all melted, cool completely. Then cover with plastic wrap and refrigerate until it has set for about 1 hour.

Put the cocoa in a bowl for rolling.

Scoop out teaspoons of the set truffle mixture and roll each in your hands to make a ball.

Coat the balls with the cocoa.

Put them in the fridge to firm up for about 30 minutes. Dust them with cinnamon before serving.

Top Tip • You can flavor these with cinnamon, salt, or chilli too. You can also coat them with coconut, confectioners' sugar, or sprinkles.

Vegan Coconut Ice Cream

Personally, I think homemade ice cream is the best, because I know exactly what's gone into it, and I can make the flavors I love without trying to find them in the store. Coconut is both hydrating and cooling, which makes it the perfect ice cream ingredient. This ice cream is light and soft, so it scoops beautifully, and all you need is a can of coconut milk!

Serves 4-6

14 ounces (400 g) canned coconut cream

½ cup (100 g) sugar

2 heaped tablespoons (30 ml) coconut oil, melted

seeds from 1 vanilla pod

Freeze the inside container of your ice cream maker overnight before making the ice cream.

Place all the ingredients into a bowl and whisk together until it's fully incorporated. Cover and refrigerate for 30 minutes.

Put the mixture into the chilled bowl of the ice cream maker, and churn for about 20 minutes until it's thick.

Pour into a container and set in the freezer for about 2 hours.

Top Tip • If you don't have an ice cream maker, you can still make this: Just pour the final mixture into a tub and pop it into the freezer. Every 30 minutes, for 4 hours, remove it and give it a good mix to aerate and distribute ice crystals.

Rose Kulfi

Kulfi is the Indian answer to ice cream, but the flavor is slightly different. Traditional Western ice cream uses a method of whipping or aerating a mixture of milk or cream, eggs, and sugar, then freezing it. To make kulfi, you heat full-fat milk until it reduces to about one-third of the original volume. This produces a thick and creamy mixture that can then be flavored with fruit purées, nuts, or spices. This is poured into molds and frozen. As a result, the kulfi is denser and richer than most ice cream.

Makes 4-6

7 ounces (200 g) raspberries for a purée

½ lime

1 tablespoon sugar

¾ to 1 cup (200 ml) double cream or heavy cream

⅔ cup (200 g) sweetened condensed milk

2 to 3 tablespoons (14 to 21 g) chopped pistachios, more for garnish

1 tablespoon edible rose petals (optional), more for garnish

1 teaspoon rose water

frozen berries

For the purée, place the raspberries into a pan with a squeeze of lime and the sugar. Heat on medium heat until the raspberries break down, and strain out the seeds. Cool.

Put the cream, condensed milk, pistachios, rose petals (if using), rose water, and raspberry purée into a large mixing bowl and mix until fully combined.

Pour the rose-colored mixture into silicone molds and place in the freezer for at least 4 hours.

Pop the frozen kulfi out of the molds at least 15 minutes before serving, and finish with chopped pistachios, frozen berries, and rose petals.

Chaat Wala Fruit

As children, we would usually have fruit as a dessert—simple, healthy, and delicious too. We had ours plain, but the grown-ups would always cover their fruit in salt, pepper, chilli, and a whole lot of other weird stuff. I didn't get it at the time, but I grew up to love it. It may sound odd—fried potatoes and fruit with spices—but honestly, give it a try!

Serves 4-6

2 tablespoons (30 ml) oil

1 sweet potato, boiled, peeled, and diced

1 potato, boiled until soft and diced

2 oranges, peeled and chopped into chunks

1 large mango, peeled, pitted, and diced

1 green apple, cored and diced

1 teaspoon chaat masala

1 teaspoon cumin seeds, toasted and crushed

½ teaspoon red chili powder

½ teaspoon black salt

2 tablespoons (30 ml) lemon juice

10 mint leaves, sliced

Heat the oil in a pan over medium to high heat and fry the diced potatoes until crisp. Place on paper towels to drain.

Place the prepared fruit in a large bowl. Add the crispy potatoes.

Mix the spices together and sprinkle over the fruit and potatoes. Add the lemon juice and toss. Check and adjust the seasoning if required.

Add the mint leaves and serve.

Pistachio Praline Parfait

My favorite dessert of all time! Not only is it a total delight to eat, but it's a pleasure to make as well. I don't think I've ever met anyone who doesn't like it. Keep a block of it in the freezer for those unexpected moments and unexpected guests.

Serves 4-6

vegetable oil for greasing

2 ounces (55 g) unsalted pistachios, shelled

½ cup (100 g) caster sugar

PARFAIT

2 large free-range eggs, separated

¼ cup (50 g) caster sugar

seeds from half a vanilla pod

¾ to 1 cup (200 ml) double cream or heavy cream

GARNISH

fresh raspberries

unsalted pistachios

Grease a sheet of parchment paper and put it on a tray.

Crush the pistachios with a mortar and pestle—it should be lumpy, not a fine powder.

Heat a little of the sugar on low heat in a pan. Once it dissolves, add a little more and move the pan around to help it melt. Do not use a spoon to stir it. Continue until all the sugar has melted and turns a lovely brown caramel color.

Add the pistachios and pour out onto the baking parchment paper. Don't worry if it's not all smooth; you will be breaking it up once it has set. Please be aware this is very hot and sticky, so don't touch it.

Once it has cooled and set, break it into chunks by placing it in a plastic bag and crushing it with a rolling pin.

PARFAIT

Line a 16-ounce (450 g) loaf pan with a double layer of plastic wrap, leaving a bit hanging over the edges.

Put the egg yolks, ¼ cup (50 g) caster sugar, and the seeds from the vanilla pod in a large bowl, and whisk with an electric mixer or a balloon whisk until thick and pale.

In another bowl, whip the cream to soft peaks and fold it gently into the egg yolk mixture using a balloon whisk.

Whisk the egg whites in another bowl with clean beaters or a clean balloon whisk until very stiff, then gently fold them through the creamy yolk mixture with the whisk.

Gently fold through the broken pistachio praline.

Pour into the pan and cover lightly with the overhanging plastic wrap and freeze for around 8 hours.

When ready to serve, remove the parfait from the freezer and let it soften for a few minutes. Unwrap the plastic wrap on top and use it to lift the parfait from the pan. Invert onto a serving platter, and then peel off the plastic wrap. Dip a palette knife in a mug of just-boiled water to warm it. Wipe it dry and use the flat of the knife to smooth away the marks from the plastic wrap.

Let it sit for 10 minutes to soften before slicing it. Serve scattered with fresh raspberries and extra pistachios.

Turmeric Latte

These alternative teas are super popular at the moment, and no surprise—they taste great. I have such vivid memories of my mum making something like this, a small sweet tonic given to the kids and the grandparents, usually before bedtime. Turmeric is a wonder spice, with so many amazing benefits, from reducing inflammation to aiding digestion.

A few words of wisdom: Always grate fresh turmeric with gloves on, as it stains everything. Pepper is an important component here, as it is required by your body to aid the absorption of turmeric. Luckily, you no longer need to spend a fortune at your local coffeehouse!

Makes 4 cups

1 cup (240 ml) unsweetened almond milk or coconut milk beverage

1 tablespoon fresh turmeric, grated

2 teaspoons maple syrup or honey

1 teaspoon fresh ginger, grated

freshly ground black pepper

dusting of cinnamon or a cinnamon stick to garnish

Blend the milk, turmeric, maple syrup (or honey), ginger, and pepper on high in a blender until smooth.

Pour into a small saucepan and heat over medium-high heat until steaming hot but not boiling. Pour into a mug and garnish with cinnamon.

Top Tip • If you use cow's milk, make sure that you use ground spices rather than fresh or your milk will curdle—¼ teaspoon ground turmeric, ¼ teaspoon ground cinnamon, ¼ teaspoon ground ginger, and a bit of ground black pepper.

Blue Moon Milk

Warm milk has long been used as a sleep aid. Moon milk is a varietal that uses key Ayurvedic herbs for well-being. My grandma told me that in India they'd drink the milk from cows that were milked at night; I now realize that this is because it contains higher levels of tryptophan and melatonin, both of which aid relaxation and rest. Interestingly, some nut milks also naturally contain these chemicals. Moon milk can be a simple preparation of milk and honey or a rich infusion of herbs and warming spices. Either way, it's about calming the nervous system and helping the body prepare for sleep.

Some good plant milk options include almond and oat milk, which contain melatonin, tryptophan, and magnesium. Cashew milk and coconut milk are also rich in magnesium and have a lovely, creamy texture that works beautifully in moon milk.

There are lots of herbs you can use to aid sleep, but many, like valerian, are strong in flavor. Some good alternatives include ashwagandha (Indian ginseng), which is known to reduce stress and anxiety. Chamomile is a calming agent familiar to most people. And butterfly pea flower is an herb that's been used for centuries in Southeast Asia to ease feelings of restlessness and help the body unwind from stress. As a bonus, it leaves a sleepy blue hue to the milk.

Makes 4 cups

1¼ cups (300 ml) milk of choice (cow's milk, almond, coconut, cashew, oat)

¼ teaspoon ashwagandha powder

3 tablespoons dried butterfly pea flower tea (loose herb)

½ teaspoon vanilla extract

maple syrup or raw honey, to taste

1 to 2 teaspoons melted ghee or coconut oil (optional)

Add milk to a small saucepan. Sprinkle in the ashwagandha powder and whisk until well combined. Add the butterfly pea flower and vanilla extract and stir again.

Heat the milk to a simmer, and then remove from the heat.

Stir in the maple syrup or honey and cover the pan with a lid. Steep for 5 to 10 minutes.

Stir in the ghee or coconut oil. Strain into a glass and sip away.

Top Tip • To make golden moon milk instead, add ½ teaspoon turmeric, ¼ teaspoon ginger, and ¼ teaspoon cinnamon, and replace the butterfly pea flower with chamomile.

Acknowledgments

This book practically wrote itself, but it's been powered by years and years of love, guidance, and innovation by everyone who surrounds me! When you love what you do, it's easy to write about it.

I grew up in an amazing extended family and we all "loved" to eat! The joy that food and cooking brings was instilled in me by having the most fabulous foodie mum; an amazingly supportive dad, who taught us all we can do anything; siblings and incredible uncles who made me fight for my supper (I was the youngest); loving family friends who we shared meal times with; a husband and children who critique and finesse my cooking efforts; and true friends who are always up for sharing constructive feedback!

Jeremy, Neyha, and Jai, I thank you for being my best and most honest supporters, my chief tasters, my sous chefs, and everything in between—I love you!

They say a picture tells a thousand words, and with each and every exquisite shot Mark Deeprose has taken of my dishes over the years, his creative flare has left me lost for words—I thank you for your advice, patience, and the incredible way you see my food!

Mr. and Mrs. P, your unwavering support on every step of the journey, always joyful and done with so much love.

My editor Emily and the team at Quarto have been a guiding light through this whole process.

And finally, to all the amazing ladies that have lifted and empowered me over the years—my Mummyji, my Chachijis, all my sisters, the nanas, my dears, my girls, and the grand lady—thank you, thank you, thank you!

About the Author

HARI GHOTRA is a home-taught chef with a passion for sharing her love of Indian food. Following a career in marketing, Hari began teaching small groups of foodie fans how to create and enjoy authentic Indian cooking and spent several years training at the Michelin-starred Tamarind collection of restaurants. She is the author of *The Easy Indian Slow Cooker Cookbook: Prep-and-Go Restaurant Favorites to Make at Home* and *500 Curries*. She sells her own custom range of curry kits and recipe sauces designed to keep your cooking as easy as possible. She runs the biggest Indian food platform in the U.K. (harighotra.co.uk), is a regular contributor to The Daily Meal, and has been featured in *The Independent* and *The Guardian* and on CNN and Eater. She now has a global audience and regularly shares recipe on her app and YouTube channel. As the food and beverage manager for an international airline, she works with chefs around the world to create fun and exciting food concepts. Follow her on her YouTube channel: @Hari Ghotra.

Index

Indian for Everyone

Index

Inspiring | Educating | Creating | Entertaining

Brimming with creative inspiration, how-to projects, and useful information to enrich your everyday life, Quarto Knows is a favorite destination for those pursuing their interests and passions. Visit our site and dig deeper with our books into your area of interest: Quarto Creates, Quarto Cooks, Quarto Homes, Quarto Lives, Quarto Drives, Quarto Explores, Quarto Gifts, or Quarto Kids.

First Published in 2023 by Fair Winds Press, an imprint of The Quarto Group,
100 Cummings Center, Suite 265-D, Beverly, MA 01915, USA.
T (978) 282-9590 F (978) 283-2742 QuartoKnows.com

Fair Winds Press titles are also available at discount for retail, wholesale, promotional, and bulk purchase. For details, contact the Special Sales Manager by email at specialsales@quarto.com or by mail at The Quarto Group, Attn: Special Sales Manager, 100 Cummings Center, Suite 265-D, Beverly, MA 01915, USA.

27 26 25 24 23   1 2 3 4 5

ISBN: 978-0-7603-7717-8

Digital edition published in 2023
eISBN: 978-0-7603-7718-5

Library of Congress Cataloging-in-Publication Data is available.

Design and page layout: Laura Shaw Design
Cover Image: Mark Deeprose
Photography: Mark Deeprose, Thomas Alexander, and Shutterstock on pages 13, 27, 43, 50, 63, 85, 108, 113, and 114

Printed in China